STEPHEN
CRANE'S
ARTISTRY

STEPHEN CRANE'S ARTISTRY

Frank Bergon

COLUMBIA UNIVERSITY PRESS

New York and London

THE ANDREW W. MELLON FOUNDATION,
through a special grant,
has assisted the Press in
publishing this volume.

Frank Bergon is a member of the English Department at Vassar College.

LIBRARY OF CONGRESS CATALOGING IN PUBLICATION DATA
BERGON, FRANK.
  STEPHEN CRANE'S ARTISTRY.
  BIBLIOGRAPHY: P. 165
  INCLUDES INDEX.
  1. CRANE, STEPHEN, 1871–1900—CRITICISM
AND INTERPRETATION.   I. TITLE.
PS 1449.C85Z556   818'.4'09   75-19159
ISBN 0-231-03905-0
COPYRIGHT © 1975 COLUMBIA UNIVERSITY PRESS
PRINTED IN THE UNITED STATES OF AMERICA
10 9 8 7 6 5 4 3 2

FOR MY MOTHER

❖ AND ❖

FATHER

PREFACE

——•——

It should be a well-known fact that, all over the world, the engine-driver is the finest type of man that is grown. He is the pick of the earth. He is altogether more worthy than the soldier and better than the men who move on the sea in ships. He is not paid too much, nor do his glories weight his brow, but for outright performance carried on constantly, coolly, and without elation by a temperate, honest, clear-minded man he is the further point. And so the lone human at his station in a cab, guarding money, lives and the honor of the road, is a beautiful sight. The whole thing is aesthetic.

THE SCOTCH EXPRESS

This book is concerned with Stephen Crane's habit of imagination as it declares itself throughout his work—that personal quality of awareness which informs his work and makes it uniquely his own. Some of the best recent literary criticism has tried to locate and dis-cover general ways of talking about this aspect of art, an aspect which has been referred to metaphorically as a writer's unique "sig-nature," "presence," "personal voltage," and "performance." We are here concerned with how a writer reveals himself regardless of particular choices of subject and theme, or the varied philosophies, formal properties, and stylistic oddities that may differ from work to work. We are looking for the "voltage," as Seán O'Faoláin says, which "does something to the material. It lights it up; it burns it up; it makes it fume in the memory as an aroma or essence." [1] It is what draws us back to a writer in anticipation of renewed pleasure even when we already can easily paraphrase his "story," "theme," and "ideas." In Crane's case it is related to a peculiar mode of perception and projection which determines the expressive vitality of his work.

So much of Crane's fiction and poetry is composed of sudden and unusual, almost spectral, scenes, gestures, characters, sensations, and perceptions; the reader's immediate realization is that the result—if anything at all—is, as J. C. Levenson properly called it, "realism with a difference." [2] The recognition of this unearthly, hauntingly apparitional aspect of Crane's writing has led commentators, including Hemingway, to speak of Crane's art in terms of dreams and dream images. As John Berryman points out, there is also a curious transmigration as "Mountains, trees, dogs, men, horses, and boats flash in and out of each other's identities." [3] Crane specifically underscores his intended effects when he describes characters with such phrases as the "spectral soldier" [4] or as having "something of the quality of an apparition" (V, 53). But it is primarily his autonomic imagery that (to place H. L. Mencken's phrase about Crane in a new context) strikes the reader like a "flash of lightning out of a clear winter sky." [5] The cumulative result of these images, characters, and scenes is that a reading of Crane is "so like a spectral dissolution, that a witness could have wondered if he dreamed."

This last quotation is borrowed not from a critic but from a Crane story, "The Clan of No-Name" (VI, 122), and it is only one of the many instances in which Crane serves as his own best commentator. He often refers to the creative effort at work in his stories, and these references are usually more to the point than the aesthetic remarks gleaned from his letters and reported conversations. In this particular case, Crane's phrase illuminates a negative "apparitional" quality in his work. Joseph Conrad described a common reaction to Crane when he said, "I could not explain why he disappoints me—why my enthusiasm withers as soon as I close the book. While one reads, of course he is not to be questioned. He is master of his reader to the very last line—then—apparently for no reason at

all—he seems to let go his hold." [6] The criticism is not totally un-
just, but it does stop short if it lacks Conrad's thoughtful hesita-
tion, "It just occurs to me that it is perhaps my own self that is slippery. I don't know."

But it is crucial to know, as nearly as possible, which are Crane's
failings and which are those of his readers. If there is little that is
conventionally solid in Crane's fiction—if there is no strong representation of a coherent vision, no logical accumulation of some patterned movement that lingers in the mind after the work is read—
then the reader is hard pressed to wonder whether these astonishing performances deserve the attention and respect we re-
serve for the most fully realized art. But as I hope to show, some of
Crane's elusiveness may be due to our own failings as readers,
trapped into seeing only what our critical terminology allows us to
see. Conrad's remarks, I think, accurately point to Crane's formal
deficiencies without damaging his particular triumphs. It seems to
me that the self-imposed limitations of Crane's art bear the precise
responsibility for his simultaneous success and failure.

As early as 1896, Frank Norris directed readers to Crane's special
"habit and aptitude for making phrases. . . . In ordinary hands the
tale of Maggie would be 'twice-told.' " [7] Much criticism, despite its
token acknowledgment of Norris's observation, continues to spe-
cialize in abstracts of *what* happens in a novel such as *Maggie*,
rather than beginning with the *manner* in which Crane says things
happen. One result of this method is that "moral" or "ontological"
crises rise in importance; and as Crane's characters are censured for
their moral obtuseness and their lack of perception, readers project
their own moralism onto Crane. For example, it is now fashionable
(and correct) to point out that the subject of *Maggie* cannot be
Maggie herself; her story is central to only about half of the novel's
nineteen chapters. No longer is there much value in citing Crane's
famous inscription to Hamlin Garland about making "room in
Heaven for all sorts of souls (notably an occasional street girl)" (*Letters*, p. 14). Maggie, along with Crane's social criticism, becomes
secondary to what is now considered the novel's main concern. Attention shifts to Pete, Jimmie, and Mrs. Johnson, and a new Crane
remark is put to work: "the root of Bowery life is a sort of coward-

ice" (*Letters*, p. 133). We now learn that *Maggie* exposes "the loud and offensive falsity of weaklings not brave enough to face up to the dishonesty of their own actions." [8] The statement is not untrue, but it is insufficient.

And it is smug. Even to begin talking about Crane in social and moral terms is to make assumptions that his art calls into question. Crane's talent was to go over the wall to that side of experience where the spirit is quick to panic, where standards and values by which we think we live are no longer stable or even appropriate. To sit back in judgment of a Bowery world which "has become a meaningless round of temporary gratifications by hypocrites too stupid and too dishonest even to desire an escape from the cycle of their own moral cowardice" [9] is to miss that aspect of *Maggie* which keeps a commonplace novel alive—those moments when Crane approaches what was to grace his art at its best, those moments when the tale confuses, humbles, and implicates both the reader and the teller of the tale himself. The opening chapter of *Maggie* draws us into a realm of experience where normal frames of reference are immediately shaken. It is closer to hell than war, and equally otherworldly. We become trapped between repulsion and fascination, in a state of uncertainty. Not only are we in a strange world, but in that world we become strangers to ourselves. This is what is shocking about the first chapter of *Maggie*, and what produces the novel's "shock value." For a commentary on this book, it would seem better to turn to another Crane story rather than to the letter in which he speaks of the cowardice of Bowery life. In "An Experiment in Misery," a young man has gone through the same kind of shock as the reader of *Maggie* may feel.

> "Well," said the friend, "did you discover his [the tramp's] point of view?"
> "I don't know that I did," replied the young man, "but at any rate I think mine own has undergone a considerable alteration." [VIII, 863]

To apprehend how Crane effects this alteration of perspective and its subsequent—if only momentary—alteration of sensibility is to move close to that distinguishing habit of imagination which informs his best work. His virtue as a writer lies in the full attention given to the scene or mood at hand, no matter how it relates to common conceptions of experience. His is an effort to treat seriously and significantly every selected detail until that detail, or the scene of which it is part, blossoms into a thing strange and new, often at the expense of a larger design or even of the dominant subject. He writes until one of those "short, terse epigrams struck off in the heat of composition," [10] or a turn of phrase, or a surrealistic image, or even a striking word within a sentence, produces the desired aura of strangeness necessary to bend the reader's angle of vision. The reader now looks upon reality metamorphosed, a world in which tents can spring up "like strange plants" and campfires can dot the night "like red, peculiar blossoms" (RB, 212). For Crane the "real thing" [11] often seems not to be somewhere awaiting his discovery but rather a creation of his imagination, wrenched into existence. This activity and its effect are the main concern of this book, for it is this aspect of Crane's artistry that seems most often to astonish us into a search for words to describe his peculiar authority as a writer. Even Henry James, at times, could only say over and over again. "He has great, great genius." [12]

Acknowledgment is made to the following for permission to use copyrighted material: Harcourt Brace Jovanovich, Inc. for lines from "Preludes" by T. S. Eliot; Cooper Square Publishers, Inc. for poems and lines from The Poems of Stephen Crane: A Critical Edition, edited by Joseph Katz; Little, Brown and Co. for lines from The Complete Poems of Emily Dickinson, edited by Thomas H. Johnson, copyright © 1914, 1942 by Martha Dickinson Bianchi. The completed volumes of the Virginia edition of The Works of Stephen Crane, edited by Fredson Bowers, are used as texts for most of Crane's work.

I would like to thank Donald Pizer of Tulane University and Anne Alexander for reading portions of the manuscript, Kathy Taylor for tracking down citations and proofreading, Holly St. John Neil for making the index, Zeese Papanikolas for offering helpful suggestions, and Karen Mitchell of Columbia University Press for guiding the book to its final form. My special thanks goes to Warner Berthoff of Harvard whose example as a teacher and writer inspired this approach to Crane's artistry.

CONTENTS

STEPHEN CRANE'S ARTISTRY

VOICES OF PERCEPTION: CRANE'S PROSE STYLE

It was like a blow in the chest to the wide-eyed volunteer. It revealed to him a point of view.   DEATH AND THE CHILD

No American writer of fiction before the twentieth century forged a closer stylistic approximation of immediate sensory and perceptual experience than did Stephen Crane. Whether consciously or unconsciously, Crane made a point of presenting the emotional qualities of those sensations and perceptions, and as if this were not enough, it seems that he also expected his prose to go beyond description and to excite immediate emotional response. These tasks were assigned to prose that was seemingly of the greatest verbal and syntactic simplicity. The result, however, was a complex welter of narrative voices. Crane wished his fiction to be a "substitute for nature" (*Letters,* p. 31) or reality, a fiction that rendered the components of experience with a local intensity and yet with enough perspective so that those components might be measured from a large, indifferent, and often nonhuman point of view. Ironically, though he worked to "approach the nearest to nature and truth" (*Letters,* p. 31), he wrote in a way that still strikes readers as contrived and unnatural. A close look at his prose led A. J. Liebling to observe that "Crane did not 'reproduce the immediacies of battle'; he made a patterned, a rhetorical, war such as never existed." [1] But that rhetorical war became an experience in itself, a substitute experience perhaps, but nevertheless an experience fashioned as a paradigm of the original. A paradox of Crane's writing, then, is that while he manipulated language for the sake of faithfully rendering experience in its immediacy, his peculiar arrangement of words often stylized experience and imparted to it a curious aesthetic distance. His words and their arrangement—the literary display of Crane's personality—remain so forcibly peculiar that his prose style is normally viewed as one of the most idiosyncratic of the nineteenth century.

John Berryman suggests that there are three basic variations, or "norms," of Crane's narrative style.[2] The first norm is "flexible, swift, abrupt, and nervous," which describes the prose written after Crane's so-called clever period. It is essentially the prose of *The Red Badge of Courage.* Though it is impossible to know exactly what Berryman meant by these impressionistic epithets, one can discriminate in Crane's prose certain procedures and effects which match common conceptions of the words. The flexibility of *The Red Badge* is evident when compared with the stiffness of Crane's first novel, *Maggie,* in which most of the ironic effects are inherent in the drama or easily achieved through mixed diction. Variations of the narrative voice do occur in *Maggie,* but usually only after long intervals (the first major change in voice occurs after chapter 3) and never in the extreme fashion that they do in his war novel. While Crane usually *reports* the perceptions and dim thoughts of his Bowery characters, he more often *presents* those of Henry Fleming. The fundamental difference in effect between these methods of narration is that while the narrator (or observer) of *Maggie* is not obtrusive, he is more often present than is the narrator of *The Red Badge.* In the war novel, rendition for the most part supplants narration, and the range of observation moves from the scenic to immediate perception and thought. The speed with which Crane moves from one subject to another is certainly "swift"; effects or visualizations are accomplished quickly and abandoned as soon as they are realized. But it is the sudden and often illogical transitions between effects or subjects that point to the most important traits of this prose, its "nervousness" and "abruptness." Usually paragraphs are as brusque as the sentences which form them. The words and their arrangement correspond to their most general subject, which—to borrow a line from "The Upturned Face"—"had its origin in that part of the mind which is first moved by the singing of the nerves" (VI, 298). At times, brief paragraphs, composed of one or two sentences, rapidly present successive sensations, appearances, and fantasies; at other times they duplicate the uncontrolled turnings, the "thousand details of color and form" (RB, 224) impressed upon an agitated mind; and in these turnings, the normal structure of language breaks down. Often, however, each paragraph has its own logic once a new point of departure is established. The suddenness of a transition is occasionally reinforced by an unexpected word or image in the opening sentence: "The guns squatted in a row like savage chiefs" (RB, 228). The thematic words, "guns" and "chiefs," trigger the development to follow: "They argued with abrupt violence. It was a grim pow-wow." Development continues until the arbitrarily invented theme is exhausted, in this case in the next sentence, "Their busy servants ran hither and thither." If Crane did not also use "hither and thither" in the opening sentences of other paragraphs, those words might reflect the slackening imagination which produced them; as it is, they indicate the slackening theme. Then a new beginning and subject take over: "A small procession of wounded men were [sic] going drearily toward the rear." The procession, too, is transformed: "It was a flow of blood from the torn body of the brigade." And, again, the paragraph abruptly ends. An implicit cause-and-effect relationship, however, has been established between these seemingly disconnected paragraphs, and both are absorbed in an overriding theme, the savagery of battle.

This style invites a qualifying epithet, "shortwinded." It also might be called "claustrophobic," for the point of view is mostly Henry's, or else it is restricted to a close-up view of the boy himself ("Into the youth's eyes there came a look that one can see in the orbs of a jaded horse"; RB, 230). Less often, the narrative presents what could be called the regiment's point of view. Only the actual sentences of the novel are out of the boy's reach; the memories and associations from which they are drawn ("savage chiefs," "grim pow-wow") are within the realm of his past experiences or fantasies, likely components of a young boy's consciousness.

Later, as Crane experimented with observations less restricted to a limited consciousness, his style opened toward Berryman's second norm, the "supple majesty of 'The Open Boat.' " Though unexpected figurative language continues to spark the prose, the figures are often not only thematically resonant but integral to a developing occasion. For example, the sentence in "The Open Boat," "It was less to him than the breaking of a pencil's point" (V, 85) is more than just a cute statement. It appropriately expresses the correspondent's former indifference to an imaginary soldier's plight. In addition, the action of the image also shares the time reference established by the entire paragraph—youthful schooldays, when the breaking of pencils and the reading of sentimental poems occur with similar regularity and elicit similar responses. In general the prose of the second norm is more flexible, less abrupt than the first. The relentless intensity of *The Red Badge*, maintained by sheer willful invention, is replaced by a prose that achieves intensity through contrast and modulation, and is marked by the increased use of statements totally devoid of exaggerated emotion or physical sensation.

The third norm is "much more closed, circumstantial and 'normal' in feeling and syntax" than the second. Understandably, it is the style of "The Monster," where the primary frame of reference is not the sea or war but society. The prose adapts to the type of information it provides; and from the reader's point of view, the chief purpose of the prose is again one of narration as well as stimulation.

These variations of Crane's style are neither strictly chronological nor mutually exclusive. The boy who, in 1892, wrote, "They regarded the little man with eyes that made wheels revolve in his soul" (VIII, 241), became the man who, in 1897, wrote, "the Swede fizzed like a fire-wheel" (V, 154). The general shift from mannered to plain prose represents, in certain instances, a mastery of craft, an economy of statement, and a variation in point of view rather than a profound change of intention. There is little doubt of the shared evocative and thematic intentions of these passages from works published in 1895 and 1900, respectively:

The ranks opened covertly to avoid the corpse. The invulnerable dead man forced a way for himself. The youth looked keenly at the ashen face. The wind raised the tawny beard. It moved as if a hand were stroking it. He vaguely desired to walk around and around the body and stare; the impulse of the living to try to read in dead eyes the answer to the Question. *[RB, 217]*

"Yes," he said, "we'd better see . . . what he's got." He dropped to his knees and approached his hands to the body of the dead officer. But his hands wavered over the buttons of the tunic. The first button was brick-red with drying blood, and he did not seem to dare to touch it.

"Go on," said the adjutant hoarsely.

Lean stretched his wooden hand, and his fingers fumbled bloodstained buttons. . . . At last he arose with a ghastly face. He had gathered a watch, a whistle, a pipe, a tobacco pouch, a handkerchief, a little case of cards and papers. He looked at the adjutant. There was a silence. The adjutant was feeling that he had been a coward to make Lean do all the grizzly business. *[VI, 297–98]*

The selection from *The Red Badge* gives a hint—if only a hint—of the excesses of the early style, while the passage from "The Upturned Face" hints at the occasional flagging in Crane's later style when the language of a mentality familiar to the reader replaces the invented tropes of a sensibility remote from the reader's own.[3] But both passages present a product of Crane's skill that transcends the excesses and impoverishments of his styles.

Fiction such as this, which is immediate, concentrated, vivid, and intense, is everywhere evident in Crane's work; supportive examples can be drawn at random from any of his three "norms." Much of this style, of course, was really the style of the times. Even if Caroline Gordon is only half correct in saying, "Since Stephen Crane's time, all serious writers have concentrated on the effort of rendering individual scenes more vividly," [4] her reference to "Crane's time" must still remind us that his prose techniques were not his alone. In fact, verbal procedures used by Crane, such as "Inversions, odd conjunctions of words, syntax set awry, these were all devices James employed to bring his prose—composed as it was of ordinary diction—alive." [5]

What, then, was Crane's, and Crane's alone? For one thing, there was his distinctive use of these devices. But more importantly, as should become clear, the linguistic effects of these devices coincided naturally with the interpretive processes of his imagination. In general, as fictional effects in Crane's time became concentrated, individual words and phrases rose in importance; diction was simplified and made concrete; syntax followed suit, and as it too became simpler, it fell apart. Harold Martin and Richard Bridgman have both shown that this change in American prose was neither sudden nor arbitrary.[6] The gradual incorporation of everyday speech into literary language affected more than the diction of prose. As Bridgman shows, stylization of the colloquial resulted in "a) stress on the individual verbal unit, b) a resulting fragmentation of syntax, and c) the use of repetition to bind and unify."[7] All three characteristics are evident in Crane's Bowery dialect:

> "Dere she stands, . . . Dere she stands! Lookut her! Ain' she a dindy? An' she was so good as to come home t'her mudder, she was! Ain' she a beaut'? Ain' she a dindy?" [I, 64]

Even the more subtle development of these characteristics of speech, as found in Crane's narrative passages, is not unique to him. Indeed, the phenomenon has a long history; Aristotle observed that "Art is cleverly concealed when the speaker chooses his words from ordinary language and puts them together like Euripides, who was the first to show the way."[8] For the moment, the achievement of other American writers' colloquial style is not central to the discussion of how or why Crane bent language to suit his own needs. Negative definitions of his purpose appear in his fiction as comments on the public's reluctance to accept, or art's failure to provide, the "real thing." In *George's Mother* he describes an avenue's "deep bluish tint which is so widely condemned when it is put into pictures" (I, 115). The protagonist of "One Dash—Horses," while escaping from Mexican bandits, "remembered all the tales of such races for life, and he thought them badly written" (V, 22). In rejecting literary styles which Crane identified with the false and badly written, he most noticeably abandons long, complex sentences possessing clear transitions. Perhaps he rejected these connections, within and between sentences, because they present extended opportunities for commentary, moralisms, and interpretations, and they place a verbal screen between the reader and the occasion of interest. Directness of expression, however, risks boring the reader with its willful limitation of syntactical forms and vocabulary. It has to make up for what it lacks in variety, mass, and movement, with intensity. Repetition is often the result, as in this paragraph from "A Dark Brown Dog," in which "dog" and "child" and their respective personal and possessive pronouns appear fifteen times:

> He stopped opposite the child, and the two regarded each other. The dog hesitated for a moment, but presently he made some little advances with his tail. The child put out his hand and called him. In an apologetic manner the dog came close, and the two had an interchange of friendly pattings and waggles. The dog became more enthusiastic with each moment of the interview, until with his gleeful caperings he threatened to overturn the child. Whereupon the child lifted his hand and struck the dog a blow upon the head. [VIII, 52–53]

Words are repeated, however, for the sake of sustained focus and accuracy. "Repetition may be bad," Mark Twain said, "but surely inexactness is worse." [9]

The passage is from an early story, but if the educated diction is excised, the bones of Crane's late, austere style can be seen. The lulling repetitions of words and sentence structures, together with the polite diction, heighten the surprise of the unexpected blow in the last sentence. Surprise, a staple of Crane's prose, is achieved in other ways as well:

> At a distance there were occasional appearances of swift-moving men, horses, batteries, flags, and, with the crashing of infantry volleys were heard, often, wild and frenzied cheers. [VI, 49]

This single sentence contains several of the verbal procedures characteristic of Crane's prose. Though sometimes awkward, these procedures are still the ones responsible for Crane's surprising "pictures" and for his way of upsetting the concepts of causality inherent in more conventional prose. Inversions often bring into immediate relief a noun or series of nouns which impress the pictorial or sensational "thing" upon the reader: "A glittering bugle swung clear of the rider's back as fell headlong the horse and the man" (VI, 48). Incidental detail, at which Crane was so adept, is often emphasized through syntactic isolation: "He faltered, and then became motionless, save for his quivering knees" (*RB*, 280). Common adjectives and adverbs also receive added force when presented out of normal sequence: "Then suddenly through the faint brown palings was stuck an envelope, white and square" (VI, 119). Likewise, after their ordeal in the open boat, the surviving men did not *then* feel they could be interpreters; rather "they felt that they could then be interpreters" (V, 92). The placement of the "then" emphasizes time rather than inevitable causality, and introduces a gap—and perhaps a discrepancy—between the experience and its interpretation. Besides these forced adjustments of language, Crane sometimes uses directional adverbs and phrases to isolate and emphasize words: "The bugle had in the west ceased" (VI, 126). Or, in the absence of specificity, they are used for their kinesthetic value: "The youth turned to look behind him and off to the right and off to the left" (*RB*, 227); "they were fighting, too, over there, and over there, and over there" (*RB*, 228). With copulas, these adverbs supply rhythmic space around nouns or gerunds of substance or action. All Crane's work is spotted with sentences beginning "There was" or "There were." The words again direct attention to the thing, situation, or action to be emphasized, like the subject in the following sentence: [10] "It thrilled the blood, this thunder" (VIII, 342). With this simplification of syntax and transparency of verbs comes a tendency to render the concrete through simple enumeration. The conjunction "and" is the usual connective, but commas or prepositions are as serviceable: "There was a shine of lanterns, of helmets, of rubber coats, of the bright, strong trappings of the horses" (VIII, 343). A vague adjective can achieve an emotional power it inherently lacks when it appears at the end of such an arithmetical list: "There was a pug dog and three old women on a bench, a man and a maid with a book and a parasol, a sea-gull drifting high in the wind, and a distant, tremendous meeting of sea and sky" (VIII, 16). Crane achieves much the same effect in the opening paragraph of a late story, "The Five White Mice," in which bar patrons are introduced. They serve no further function in the story, but the flat, general listing of the men by occupations builds to a description of Freddie, who "surveyed them with the ironical glance of a man who is mixing a cocktail" (V, 39). The simile is vague, but by contrast, it makes Freddie important; it throws a light on him.

The burden that Crane's writing places upon individual words also places a burden upon the reader, for though concentration of expression may be striking enough to give the reader pause, it may confuse before it illuminates. "Potter and his bride walked sheepishly and with speed. Sometimes they laughed together shamefacedly and low" (V, 118). These adverbial units are under pressure to convey much information, but by their nature, they serve two other functions indicative of Crane's style. Like isolated notes, they supply a tone, an emotion, to the scene; and their repetitive cadences relax tension. Without such devices Crane's prose would have no modulation. In the sentence quoted earlier from *The Red Badge* ("At a distance there were occasional appearances of swift-moving men, horses, batteries, flags"), the syntactical dislocations successfully jar the reader's expectations. But a ceaseless rush of such "appearances" would not produce even Crane's desired effect of "an instant's picture" (VI, 48) if his prose did not slacken enough to place a border around the picture. So Crane's fiction is filled with what Yeats would call "numb lines," lines which may be unexceptional in themselves but which, by contrast, heighten the lines before or after. Words may be numb too; they provide spaces in which both writer and reader can breathe. "Hither and thither" is one example already mentioned. Others are general stage directions that may appear as a paragraph in themselves—"The woman waved her hand" (I, 59), or "Maggie went away" (I, 67).[11] Perhaps one of the more personal manifestations of this technique is the use of parallel, curiously redundant statements, which span Crane's career: "The fence was there and it stopped his progress. He could not go in that direction" (VI, 106); or, "The man was playing with this town. It was a toy for him" (V, 118). It is possible to relate these characteristics to normal speech patterns, but the cadences achieved by numb lines, parallelism, and even the repetition of words, phrases, and rhythms are also solidly biblical.

In a style as fragmented as Crane's, cohesion is what is most often missed. Bits of prose, made up of individual words or phrases, no matter how concentrated, vivid, or even mesmerizing, are still essentially bits of prose. Crane's compensatory strategy, much like the Bible's or the strategy of primitive verse, is to bypass normal syntactic connectives and relate sentences and phrases through subtle variations of repetition, the very means that tends to emphasize them and thus isolate them from larger, more coherent verbal structures. A key word may establish the dominant tone or mood of a paragraph (or several paragraphs), as the word "quiet" does before the fire breaks out in the sixth section of "The Monster" (VII, 20). A more subtle form of repetition, though hardly consistently conscious, links words through their sounds. Almost any page offers them; "sea of snow" (V, 144), "all grim and of ghastly shape" (VI, 97), "glossy sides of galloping horses" (VIII, 343), "wail of its whistle" (VIII, 343), "smoke, sprinkled thickly with sparks" (VIII, 344). Less colloquial and more important to Crane's style is his tendency to bind sentences by a series of synonyms rather than by exact repetition. Even when the logical movement from sentence to sentence borders on the incoherent (as when the mind is agitated), one word and a series of synonyms chain the sentences together. Four sentences in chapter 12 of *The Red Badge* achieve cohesion by the successive appearance of "dusk," "day had faded," "purple darkness," and "blue and somber sky" (*RB*, 253), and yet this tonal painting is secondary to the focus of the scene, which is Fleming's movement toward a group of men who are jabbering and gesticulating against this backdrop.

Despite these fragile linguistic connectives, the emphasis in Crane's prose is still upon units of expression which, in their separateness, demand an attention of their own. The result is a series of appearances, which are abrupt, often elliptical, usually sequential and linear. Actions and events, like things and characters, find their most suitable presentation through simple sentences or syntactic units joined by connective conjunctions. But even in Crane's later style, where sentences of greater length and complexity are more common—as in the long sentence in "The Monster" describing Trescott's drive home—there remains a sequential movement from action to action. Trescott drives home, smokes a cigar, hears a fire whistle, chirps to his horse, and thinks that there is a fire but considers it to be some distance from his own home, all in one sentence (VII, 25). When faced with Crane's vivid prose, the reader often must become much like the Easterner in "The Blue Hotel," whose "mind, like a film, took lasting impressions" (V, 159); but according to Crane, the virtues of these impressions, whether lasting or transitory, must exceed the virtues of the photograph. "The photograph," he wrote, "is false in perspective, in light and shade, in focus. When a photograph can depict atmosphere and sound, the comparison will have some meaning" (VIII, 507).

Crane's early attempts to render atmosphere and sound are bizarre. In the Sullivan County tales and sketches, the woods are always singing, crying, purring, crooning, whispering, or sighing. Even in his later prose, Crane tried to duplicate as well as describe sound. He wrote of the "mellow clash—clash—clash" of spurs (V, 19), and how, while filling a grave, "the earth made that sound—plop" (VI, 300). He stressed the "prut" of magazine rifles (VI, 109) and the "whiroo" of a shark's fin as it flashed through water (V, 84). In a late work, "The Lone Charge of William B. Perkins," these typographical equivalents became extreme. Reference is made to the "old familiar *flut-flut-fluttery-fluttery-flut-flut-flut* from the entrenchments" (VI, 115–16) and to the "*Sss-s-s-swing-sing-ing-Pop*" of bullets (VI, 116). But sound in prose achieves its most effective realization through speech. Crane is noted for his studied reproductions of dialect—such as Irish: "Shure, if yez got for th' askin', 'tis you, Mickey, that would niver be in want" (VIII, 493); or Cuban: "You have insult me. I must have s-s-satisfact-shone. . . . If you touch me wis your hand, I will keel you. . . . If you touch me wis your hand, I will cut your heart in two piece" (VIII, 354–56). Accuracy of transcription might fulfill the tenets of realism, but Crane knew that speech served other purposes. The discrepancy between an emotion and its inadequate human expression enlarges the emotion and sharpens its poignancy in a way that a fully attempted expression cannot:

> The youth still lamented. "Oh, Jim—oh, Jim—oh, Jim—"
> "Yeh know," said the tall soldier, "I was out there." He made a
> careful gesture. "An', Lord, what a circus! An', b'jiminey, I got
> shot—I got shot. Yes, b'jiminey, I got shot." [RB, 240]

No amount of narrative description of "smoke-infested fields" and shrill yells can immediately dramatize the human tension at the beginning of battle as does a soldier softly mumbling, "Oh, we're in for it now!" (RB, 224). A voice not only vivifies a moment, but in the outrageous situations of Crane's fiction, where characters find themselves stranded in countries as foreign as the moon and faced with experiences equally remote, the sound of the human voice becomes a point of reference; it helps to humanize what is humanly incomprehensible.

The contrast between a situation and a character's articulation of it is only one way Crane focuses the reader's attention on what is unstated. Unlike the photograph, he selects words and shuffles syntax so as to alter the epistemological bias of normal prose, shunning the democratic reception of details through an open shutter. Even the smallest units of narrative offer examples of adjustments in perspective through contrasts of light and shade. Willa Cather stressed Crane's ability "to handle detail. . . . If he saw one thing in a landscape that thrilled him, he put it on paper, but he never tried to make a faithful report of everything else within his field of vision." [12] What Cather neglects to say is that the logic behind Crane's choice of the incidental detail is determined by "everything else within his field of vision." He turns his attention upon a gatepost in "The Blue Hotel," not because the gatepost is in any way significant but because its fixed position gives meaning and emphasis to the chaotic storm that whirls around it: "A gate-post like a still man with a blanched face stood aghast amid this profligate fury" (V, 144). Once again, the inhuman, the indifferent, is given a point of human reference. Underlying the epistemological choices of Crane's prose is this persistent habit of perception by contrast. [13] Shading in his prose is as important as lighting, and out of context, a striking incidental detail may become as dull as the side of a rainbow trout out of water. Crane's words become mutually dependent, and their selection is determined by an imagination which knows that brilliancy is relative, that what we see becomes more intense when measured by what we normally fail to see. The clarity and depth of a stream are not so noticeable until, far below, a dark trout streaks through it.

Crane's method of achieving emotional atmosphere goes beyond this pictorial effectiveness. His emotional coloring is not merely descriptive; it projects response. It is not unusual that in a storm a gatepost might look like a man, but Crane forces an observer to project himself to be that man in the storm. By this imaginative leap of logic, the gatepost now stands "aghast" amid the swirling snow. Often an adverb or adjective floats illogically in a sentence for no other reason than as an interpretive clue to guide the reader's reaction toward a particular scene. The adverb "piteously" serves this purpose when Henry Fleming looks at a corpse and notices "that the soles of his shoes had been worn to the thinness of writing paper, and from a great rent in one the dead foot projected piteously" (*RB*, 217). At times Crane is so shameless in his piling up of words for states of feeling that precision is surrendered for affective overkill: "Edified, aghast, triumphant, he paused suddenly, his lips apart" (V, 125). The sound of a snake's rattle changes a man "to a statue of listening horror, surprise, rage" (VIII, 65). More will be said about the conception of emotions underlying this habit, but for the moment it is enough to see that Crane stresses the complexity and ambiguity of feeling, particularly emotional states caused by occasions that are the opposite of normal.

All these details of expression make up a prose that may not be strictly photographic, but in a sense is cinematic. There is movement in Crane's prose, and the movement is not always from scene to scene, but often zooms in on a scene; the writing often moves from a wide-angle view to a close-up of significant details. We can now look back at the description of the corpse in *The Red Badge* and see how the sentences work like separate frames in a film. The movement of vision is from the general to the overwhelmingly particular; the words which bind the sentences together and intensify the focus are "corpse," "dead man," "ashen face," and finally "tawny beard." The wind raising the tawny beard is the contrasting detail which emphasizes the deadness of the man. Everything is cinematographic except the next sentence, which provides the scene with emotion; the beard "moved as if a hand were stroking it." Again, the inhuman is measured by the human, and this image of a living hand on a dead face only too poignantly accentuates the incomprehensible gulf that separates the living from the dead, the human from the nonhuman. The short, choppy sentences abruptly approximate the leaps by which a man grows in awareness.

Such vivid evocation of scene and mood is now so typical in modern prose that Crane's originality may easily be overlooked. Because Crane renders so many scenes of violence, it is also easy to overlook the "stroking hand" that separates him from the hardboiled Kipling-Hemingway school. Crane acknowledged his debt to Kipling, and many of Crane's effects and procedures are also present in Kipling's *The Light That Failed;* but Kipling's pose is often morally obtuse, and at times so cutely phrased that his descriptions border on the callous and even the sadistic: "he had fired his revolver into a black foam-flecked face which forthwith ceased to bear any resemblance to a face." [14] In contrast, Crane's presentation of a similar event presents death from a wounded soldier's point of view. The soldier is helpless as a guerrilla bears down on him with a machete. Grass stirs, a man appears, he looms larger as he approaches the soldier. At the last minute, though, the "young lieutenant closed his eyes, for he did not want to see the flash of the machete" (VI, 132). This scene confirms V. S. Pritchett's observation that Crane "does not look mildly into the blank expressionless features of death; but dramatically, with face half-averted." [15]

As already mentioned, one effect of Crane's fiction is that it often compels the reader to become, like Henry Fleming, "deeply absorbed as a spectator" (*RB*, 291). But in a sense, Crane tried to eliminate the camera that separated the spectator from experience. One method is his experimental entrance into his characters' minds, not only to report thoughts but to duplicate their developments and waverings. Occasionally, his expressed desire to be "unmistakable" drove him to tell the reader why he expresses a thought in a particular way: "These phrases became mixed in Bill's mind precisely as they are here mixed" (V, 56). Even more dramatic is the presentation of thought processes in terms of images. In

Maggie such images substitute for inner monologue, as in Kipling; but in a later work, such as "The Five White Mice," the seeming incoherence of the images reflects the levels at which a mind can move simultaneously. Crane also explicitly distinguishes between "unconscious" (VI, 36) and "subconscious" (VIII, 297) movements of the mind, and although his well-known use of color is everywhere evident in his descriptions of places and events, it is most unmistakable in his attempts to render sensations or psychological processes: "Kelcey fell with a yellow crash" (I, 147), or "At last, however, he had made firm rebellion against this yellow light thrown upon the color of his ambitions" (*RB*, 203).

Crane most successfully duplicates immediate experience when he gives voice to perceptions that can have no voice of their own, when he dwells in that mute land between event and human consciousness of event. It is this attempt to show how we *actually* see or feel that is responsible for much of the syntactic juggling discussed earlier. He describes things or events as they immediately strike the senses, and he occasionally follows an impression as it filters through that fabric of memories and associations and acquires a name: "Sometimes, however, on days when no heat-mist arose, a blue shape, dim, of the substance of a specter's veil, appeared in the southwest, and a pondering sheep-herder might remember that there were mountains" (V, 53). Sometimes, though, this simplest of mental deductions, the movement from "a blue shape" to "mountains," is denied, and a description begins and ends in observation. For example, in "The Open Boat," a lighthouse appears "like a little grey shadow in the sky." In the next sentence Crane strives to preserve the immediacy of this perception: "The man at the oars could not be prevented from turning his head rather often for a glimpse of this little grey shadow" (V, 74).[16] Throughout his work there are similar repetitions, through which Crane comes as close as possible to sustaining an immediate optical image. This mode of perception is childlike, primitive; but its underlying assumption is that this is the point at which perception begins, a point that people are rarely aware of and rarely remember. Ordinary descriptions automatically order and falsify, for they bypass both that tiny moment when objects strike human perception and that tiny moment when events become experience. Crane's prose emphasizes that "experience" is a relational term, and an experience cannot be regarded apart from the experiencer. Therefore, what might be seen is affected by the emotion of the observer, just as the observer's emotion is altered by what he sees. In *The Red Badge* alone there are over 350 instances, according to Sergio Perosa's count,[17] of verbs indicating perception. But the quality of many of these perceptions is described as dim or vague, for what Henry (and the reader) sees is often viewed through a distorted lens. A man's eyesight can be "shaken and dazzled by the tension of thought and muscle" (*RB*, 293).

Experience often determines the arrangement of words in Crane's prose. Since perception precedes conception, a sentence describing the movement from one to the other might also approximate that process through peculiar phrasing: "Little lines of gray smoke ribboning upward from some embers indicated the place where had stood the barn" (VI, 48–49). Sequences of sentences, too, often indicate the relationship of sensation to action; their arrangement might offer reasons for behavior quite different from those produced by a reflecting narrator. In chapter 5 of *The Red Badge*, while Fleming is thinking thoughts that he will not remember, he is experiencing the "effects of the war atmosphere—a blistering sweat, a sensation that his eyeballs were about to crack like hot stones. A burning roar filled his ears." These sensations incite a "red rage" in Henry. His immediate reaction is to fight "frantically," not for his country or his companions or even self-preservation, but "for respite for his senses" (*RB*, 225–26). Such moments are remarkable for their fidelity to immediate experience.

The fragmentation of personality which results from these descriptions is relevant to the seeming absence of characterization in Crane's fiction, but for the moment it is enough that this fragmentation strives to localize sensation. Crane's idiosyncratic epithets—forgotten feet, anxious eyes, impatient shoulder, hurried fingers—serve a similar purpose. At its most effective, such writing places the narrative point of view at the initial point of perception or sensation, as in "The Open Boat," where neither "the men" nor "they" glanced at the waves; rather "Their eyes glanced level" (V, 68).

Later, "Their back-bones had become thoroughly used to balancing in the boat" (V, 75). In "Three Miraculous Soldiers," the girl does not stare into a dark barn and feel an urge to scream; rather, "Her eyes were fixed in a stare. . . . Unconsciously her throat was arranged for a sudden shrill scream" (VI, 36). In the opening paragraph of "An Ominous Baby," a series of seemingly random sentences describes a child in terms of parts of his body and clothing. The details are chosen in a camera's-eye sequence, moving from the child's hair to his feet. All the sentences follow the same straightforward subject-verb pattern except the surprising last sentence, "From a gaping shoe there appeared an array of tiny toes" (VIII, 47). The toes are presented as the reader might see them immediately, before he automatically relates the toes to the child and integrates all the parts of his visual impressions.

The information these sentences offer, then, is first what a reader or objective observer might immediately perceive and know. Similarly, when Crane mentions an impatient shoulder, the stress upon the shoulder emphasizes it as the object from which an observer deduces that a man *appears* impatient. The visual is stressed; there is no absolute guarantee that the man is actually impatient. In other instances, when Crane presents the immediate experience from a character's point of view, the information is even more limited. There is often a discrepancy between what a person might know and what he experiences. To get as close as possible to the feelings of the experiencer, Crane even dares to represent the physical sensations of an animal, as he does in early stories as well as in late ones such as "The Bride Comes to Yellow Sky," in which a dog knows a bullet only as a "something [that] spat the ground directly before it" (V, 117). A man's mental responses may not be much different from an animal's during a fractured second of physical sensation, particularly when the man has just been shot: "Somebody punched him violently in the stomach. He thought dully to lie down and rest, but instead he fell with a crash" (VI, 111).

Crane wanted immediacy and felt experience, but he also wanted his prose to have a wider point of view. For this reason, he forgoes the narrative voice that says, "I saw, I heard, I smelled, I tasted, or I felt," even though this is the literary device most capable of compelling the reader to accept the authenticity of experience. For Crane, the singleness of tone and perception of the first-person narrator was too narrow to render the full dimensions of his imagined world. His third-person narratives are filled with seemingly objective observations which, while they bear the authority of personal witness, are also filled with quick changes in perspective that reveal the limitations of immediate perception. In "The Price of the Harness," after Nolan feels as though someone had punched him in the stomach, he lies on the hillside and disputes with his friends about the dampness of the ground beneath him. Once the scene has established dramatically the ironic contradictions between Nolan's sensations and his deductions, Crane has only to say that "He did not know he was dying. He thought he was holding an argument on the condition of the turf" (VI, 112); and this flat remark releases the swell of emotion that could find no release as long as the men lightly bantered back and forth.

As with Crane's use of the incidental detail, contrast is the determining principle behind switches in voice. These switches highlight a scene, or suddenly change a point of view so as to reveal without the necessity of explanations. A shift in voice indicating a shift in point of view often produces an opportunity for implied authorial comment, recognized only by the reader, while maintaining the illusion of objective presentation. It may also create contradiction without invalidation. Crane's skill with this method of narration is shown in the quickness with which he can dart from the panoramic to the particular and back again, as he does in "Death and the Child" or "The Open Boat." Sometimes, though, it is difficult to know exactly who is talking in a Crane sentence, whose observations are being recorded. Are they the author's, the narrator's, a character's, or those of an impersonal but all-seeing eye? It is interesting that Crane's use of the impersonal "observer" is not the point of view habitually found in realistic fiction. It is not even the camera eye, which has the habit of using the human eye as a reference point from which to determine distances and heights and to make emotional judgments. Before men flew, Crane did not hesitate to record what a bird knows when, "high in the air it surveys the world" (V, 121). When Crane's voice as the author interrupts his narrative, it often does so as parody, or simply as the game of an artist aware of the discrepancies between words and the illusions produced by words; in short, Crane reveals his role as a performer while actually performing: " 'Do you dare pursue him, — ? — ! — ! — ! — !' These lines represent terrible names, all different, used by the officer" (V, 24).

Crane may also incorporate a character's voice or perceptions within the third person. At times, a new point of view is revealed by a switch in idiom. The effect is again one of immediacy, although irony is not always absent. Indirect discourse is the simplest method of achieving this authoritative perspective. However, Crane's voice may shift immediately from narration to a character's thought without indicating a change in point of view. In "God Rest Ye, Merry Gentlemen," "Tailor was prostrate up there in the grass. Never mind. Nothing was to be done. The whole situation was too colossal" (VI, 154). The comments on Tailor's situation are not the author's, but those of a character, Little Nell. Or an idiomatic phrase may establish an opposite, distant perspective on an immediate scene and simultaneously contradict the character's point of view in the same scene, as does the reference to Henry Johnson's overformal courting scene as "a great deal of kowtow" (VII, 16). Another means of achieving distance and qualifying a character's point of view is to counter a highly emotional assertion with an impassive one.

This last method of narration is most effective when the changes in tone are subtle, but there is one controversial way Crane handles these shifts in voice that cannot be ignored even though its effectiveness is constantly called into question. His interruptions of intense narrative with trite generalizations must be considered an important characteristic of his style, if for no other reason than that they are present in his first stories as well as in his last. The apparent function of these excessively mannered, slick, pithy, sententious, obvious, or silly sentences is not out of keeping with Crane's other shifts in voice and perspective. They surprise the reader, deflate a mood, and assert a distancing point of view. They are often a way of keeping emotion in check, or of evoking greater emotion through contrast rather than through a bombastic flurry of words.

They also can complete a contour of thought or emotion by presenting a pseudosummary. They provide rhythmic variation and relax intensity of scene or mood before it grows flat. By turning an apparently tragic or pathetic situation into a comic one, they affect the reader, as Crane would say, like a shifting of scene. Finally, by contrast they often point out the hopeless inadequacy of those words which might be used if expression of a true sentiment were attempted. As they appear in his first stories, Crane's clever asides seem imitations of the pseudophilosophic aphorisms that provide *The Light That Failed* with some of its humor. Kipling writes, "It is not easy for a man of catholic tastes and healthy appetites to exist twenty-four days on fifty shillings. Nor is it cheering to begin the experiment alone in all the loneliness of London." [18] Crane follows suit in "Four Men in a Cave" (1892): "It is not well to quarrel upon a slippery incline, when the unknown is below" (VIII, 227). In "An Explosion of Seven Babies," the protagonist fears for his life when "the brown giantess, mad with rage, crashed against the fence," but at that moment Crane, as narrator, draws back and tells the reader, "It is not well to behold a woman climb a fence" (VIII, 267). [19]

In a serious piece, such as "The Open Boat," this kind of sentence comes closest to achieving what Crane demands from his prose. When he remarks that "Many a man ought to have a bath-tub larger than the boat which here rode upon the sea" (V, 68), the word "bath-tub" probably had a shock value more appreciated in the 1890s than it is today. [20] But the real surprise is when what is so intense, immediate, overwhelming, and wrong is suddenly seen from another point of view as equally small, silly, and even insignificant. The principle of choice by contrast, evident in how boats and tubs differ in their use of water, only makes the situation more ludicrous. But the point which needs stressing is that the situation is also ludicrous to the men in the boat. By saying "ought to have a bath-tub" instead of "has a bath-tub," Crane approaches the outraged cry of consciousness that often comes from his characters in moments of stress. [21] The cry is consistent with the voice that finds the waves "most wrongfully and barbarously abrupt" (the two adverbs jar with the diction of the rest of the sentence). Similarly,

while the waves remained "outrageously high" and a "menace" to
the men, the boat "was not unlike a bucking broncho"; but after
the land loomed "beautifully" out of the sea, they "rode this wild
colt of a dingey like circus men." The sentiments and images might
be those of the correspondent or a man on shore; the rhetoric,
though, is Crane's, and it consists of a simultaneous presentation of
sensible details, emotional response, and the phenomenon of consciousness as it concentrates on a specific problem while experiencing a flood of unexpected thoughts and images. Crane implies that
such a moment is not to be judged in terms of "the average experience, which is never at sea in a dingey" (V, 69); nor, for that matter,
is it to be judged in terms of experience which *has* been at sea in a
dinghy. What is in question is the effective and affective use of language, the revivification of conventional phrasing to convey the dynamics of an experience.

Language, not experience, is the key term here. Crane's reputa-
tion for "pictures" and "movement" is justified, but there remain
those characteristics of his art which are neither swift nor vivid nor
cinematic. As swift as his style may be, its dominant effect is one of
retardation. As concentrated as his effects may be, his tendency is
to diffuse the force of verbs by placing them in the passive voice or
in conditional or progressive tenses. Verbs of action are in fact out-
numbered by verbs for states of being. One result is that prose
comes close to stopping time. With his emphasis on the moment,
Crane loads his sentences with participles and gerunds that further
dissipate the concentrated energy of verbs but that describe actions
as continuing rather than completed:

> He was laughing hysterically. . . . One was swearing that he had
> been shot in the arm through the commanding general's mis-
> management. One was marching with an air imitative of some sub-
> lime drum major. Upon his features was as an unholy mixture of
> merriment and agony. [RB,237]

Even though the impact of the single detail or sentence may be sudden and final, the narrative itself advances slowly, moment by moment. Paragraphs composed of independent sentences equal in
value and content also slow down the flow of ordinary fictional,
particularly novelistic, prose. What happens in the last sentence of a

paragraph may be simultaneous with the statement of the first, as in the lead paragraph of "The Open Boat."

Although Crane's pictures are vivid, the words producing them are often visually vague and imprecise. As novelists know, this apparent contradiction is the normal condition of fiction; there is always a gap between what the reader imagines and what he reads. If, for the moment, "we follow Hume," as William Gass suggests, "we think we picture things through language because we substitute, on cue, particular visual memories of our own, and the more precisely language defines its object, the less likely are we to find a snapshot in our book to fit it." [22] At times Crane's prose makes no attempt even to supply words for which the reader, on cue, can substitute "particular" visual memories. "Pale moon" could be one of those cues which even a good novelist, pressed to get on with his story, might drop into his narrative. Crane, on the other hand, speaks of an "unassuming moon" in "The Pace of Youth." The immediate effect is not a specific picture but an apprehension of the quality of the scene in which it appears—an apprehension of the gentleness, delicacy, and humility of an adolescent love scene. There is also a radiation of emotion, a vibration of shyness. "For a long time the young man was afraid to approach the two girls." A specific picture, if there can be any at all, is the least important function of the adjective, though Crane, in this instance, seizes the opportunity to add that the moon was "faintly silver" (V, 8). At the opposite extreme, when Crane does attempt to define an object more precisely, as in the opening paragraph of "An Ominous Baby," he uses a method that still frees the reader from searching his visual memories for an appropriate snapshot; a deceleration of time allows the prose slowly to accustom the reader to an unusual apprehension, perhaps composed of a number of visual memories. The "precision" of the definition, then, is not a realistic precision but a precision of observation as determined by Crane's transformative imagination.

This particular use of language is neither strictly metaphoric nor symbolic. It does share with metaphor and symbol, though, a simultaneous compression of statement and expansion of meaning beyond normal usage, often at the expense of definite description.

In a sense it is a game with words; its effectiveness depends not so much on accurate observation as on rhetorical inventiveness. "Her mother was fat" is the normal novelistic clue that triggers a picture, but Crane says that she was fat "and commercially excited" (VI, 119). There is suggestion here, but not description. This habit of expression is probably what led Willa Cather to say that Crane was best at description when least describing.[23] Whether a reader can clearly imagine hearing Scully's "ringing jokes" (V, 152) or accurately imagine how a man might turn "toward the door in immovable silence" (V, 115) is secondary to the fact that he is made to imagine. Crane is here employing a mode of expression common to poetry. "La poésie ne consiste pas," Sainte-Beuve wrote, "à tout dire mais à tout faire rêver."

There are obvious dangers in talking about Crane's prose in terms of poetry or poetics. Philip Rahv claims that "it is simply not the case that what goes for a microscopic unit such as the lyric goes equally well for the macroscopic compositions of the writer of narrative prose." [24] The greatest abuse of this tendency to assimilate the novel to the poem has been the practice of transforming Crane's work into a collection of symbols. Still, there are aspects of Crane's prose that are simply more commonly associated with poetry than with prose, or at least with prose fiction written before the 1890s. Specifically, much of his work can be classified as microscopic. Many of his stories are read as sketches, and in his novels, a deemphasis of plot and event (in the usual sense of story line) accompanies an emphasis on the texture of the work itself. The result is a compression and concentration acquired through use of the "intensive speech proper to poetry." [25] Immediate effects are preferred to the larger cumulative effect of ordinary novelistic prose. Lacking the connective patterns of normal prose, Crane's elliptical sentences often cohere according to a timeless mode of apprehension or the associative logic of poetry. For example, the sentence, "None of them knew the color of the sky," immediately raises the question "why?" but it is not until four sentences later that it is explicitly confirmed the men are in a boat, although by then the reader is already in the middle of the effect.

Melvin Schoberlin has demonstrated that Crane's prose can occasionally be broken into acceptable verse,[26] while both W. D. Howells and Hyatt Waggoner have shown that his "lines" or "pills" ("mind you," Crane wrote, "I never call them poems myself"; *Letters*, p. 96) can as easily be written out as prose.[27] It does not follow that his prose and his verse are interchangeable; but there are similarities in the disconnection and "nervousness" of prose paragraphs and verse stanzas, in the juxtaposition of contrasting points of view, and in the tendency to present rather than interpret. In both, Crane is what Ruth Miller calls "a raconteur of disjunctive experiences." [28] In the poetry there is the forced yoking of disparate words for their suggestive rather than descriptive value ("grey and boiling street," "bashful blue," "drunken sky") and there are sometimes those vague "pictures" ("Came monsters, livid with desire").[29] Punctuation and line breaks replace the syntactical juggling of the prose, but dialogues and fragments of speech are important devices in both the prose and poetry, just as is repetition—repetition of words, phrases, and whole refrains. In some ways, the prose is surprisingly more "poetic" than the poetry; it is more highly metaphoric and daring in diction,[30] and the type of cleverness common to the prose is so lacking in the verse that one exception stands out: "And when his stick left the head of the learned bystander / It was two sticks" (*WK*, 84). (Given Crane's propensity to rebel against the traditions of narrative prose, it is only consistent that he likewise rebelled against common conceptions of poetry. The impulse to shock, to make something strange and new, naturally took a different turn in the poetry.) But the most striking difference between the prose and poetry is that there are few attempts in the poems to approximate immediate sensory and perceptual experience; [31] instead, there is a plethora of "I's," representative of an observer (though not necessarily an interpreter) who is explicitly on the scene. The tactic of having an on-the-spot observer is a necessity, for the events and situations of Crane's poetry are so fancifully bizarre that it is rarely possible to invest them with as great an "illusion of reality" through other techniques; they can only be reported.

In the distinction Crane drew between *The Red Badge* and *The Black Riders*, he makes clear that he had formed different objectives for his prose and poetry. In *The Black Riders,* his aim is "to give my ideas of life as a whole, so far as I know it" (*Letters,* p. 159). It is true that the poems affirm certain elemental attitudes, beliefs, opinions, and stances toward God, man, and the universe. All these ideas have been sifted and arranged, most admirably by Daniel Hoffman; [32] but when all is said and done, the ideas themselves are too bare and simple to be strongly engaging. What might still fascinate the contemporary reader, besides the strange events and figures of the poetry, is Crane's opinion of his own opinions as it is reflected in his poetic activity. According to Arthur Oliver, Crane once scooped up a handful of sand from the beach and tossed it into the air. " 'Treat your notions like that,' he said. 'Forget what you think about it and tell how you feel about it.' " [33] That action points to the impulse of his poetry, as much as of his prose, to record the elusive, inconclusive, nature of ideas about life:

> Once, I knew a fine song,
> —It is true, believe me,—
> It was all of birds,
> And I held them in a basket;
> When I opened the wicket,
> Heavens! they all flew away.
> I cried: "Come back, little thoughts!"
> But they only laughed.
> They flew on
> Until they were as sand
> Thrown between me and the sky.   [BR, 65]

The surprise of the poetry stems from the kind of game Crane plays with normal expectations. If the poetry gives his ideas of life as a whole, then his fundamental idea is that ideas of life as a whole cannot long be apprehended; a man may search for truth but must draw satisfaction from the search itself and from certain flashes of insight that at best can only be partial. Ruth Miller claims that Crane writes "an intellectual poetry rather than a poetry that evokes feeling, a poetry that stimulates the mind rather than arouses the heart." [34] The division seems a little too clean. While the attempt to excite emotional response may be more noticeable in Crane's prose, the prose, like the poetry, also plays with ideas and stresses the inconclusiveness of various interpretations. "The Blue Hotel" is

Crane's most successful fictional achievement of this kind of ambivalence. The poems, on the other hand, may not duplicate modes
of perception that inspire precise emotional responses, but they are
in themselves projections of feelings ranging from outrage to inert
despair. They may begin as a sort of cerebral stimulation, but the
fundamental emotion of all the poems is primitive astonishment
and awe.

The poetic characteristics of Crane's fiction, its shorthand prose,
suggestibility, shifts in perspective, slowness, and ellipses between
and within sentences often produce pictures that resemble a montage more than a film; or they resemble a film spliced together
without normal logical sequence. Like parts of a montage, the descriptions are juxtaposed so that they might be apprehended simultaneously, freed from time sequences of cause and effect; also like a
montage, they often lack a stable, realistic, spatial reference:

> In all unhandy places there were buckets, brooms, rags, and bottles.
> . . . Withered persons, in curious postures of submission to some-
> thing, sat smoking pipes in obscure corners. A thousand odors of
> cooking food came forth to the street. The building quivered and
> creaked from the weight of humanity stamping about in its bowels.
> [I, 11]

It becomes clear from this passage that much of Crane's prose is
more aptly visualized in terms of a cartoon than of a realistic film.
Certain sentences, in fact, can be read as literal descriptions of
comic strip drawings: "Words bubbled from the freckled man's
mouth" (VIII, 30). It would seem that only cartoon characters can
make "gestures, painting their agonies on the air with fingers that
twirled swiftly" (V, 121), or can be seen as "a slang phrase" (RB,
251). And surely no camera could film a "bitter insult [that] seemed
to fairly spin from his lips and crackle in the air like breaking glass"
(VIII, 355). In the poetry, too, figures and events are more readily
represented by the cartoonist's pen and brush than by the photog-
rapher's film.[35]

Because of these fantastic figures and events, one feels that one is
witnessing actions in a "far strange country" (WK, 84). Even the
sensory details of Crane's prose are so transformed that there is
often a curious absence of sensuality in his work. Those details and

syntactic wrenchings which do approximate the process of immediate experience actually create artifacts, which may serve as para-
digms of the world as it is commonly known but ultimately exist in
a realm of their own, much as does a brilliant tapestry on which a
stag hunt is frozen. Commonplace objects, campfires, streams,
rocks, umbrellas cease to exist in a normal context and are trans-
posed to a "fabric of time / Where purple becomes orange / And
orange purple" (BR, 62). The process is similar to what occurs when
a chemically dyed leaf is pressed upon paper: the veins are exposed
as if for the first time, and what is real but normally unnoticed
becomes astonishingly new, while the leaf itself is lost.

There is a concordance between these unusual visualizations and
the frequent qualifications of Crane's sentences: both move his
prose further away from the literal and definite. From first to last
Crane's excessive use of words such as "seems," "evidently," "apparently," "somewhat," "probably," "must have," and "perhaps"
produces an impression of uncertainty and authorial distance while
actually making a statement of fact ("The body seemed to bounce a
little way from the earth"; RB, 243). It is common for these hesitant
forms of expression to appear in deductive statements; in contrast,
firsthand observations or immediate, untampered perceptions are
left alone.

> Suddenly some low houses appeared squatting amid the bushes.
> The horsemen rode into a hollow until the houses rose against the
> sombre sundown sky, and then up a small hillock, causing these
> habitations to sink like boats in the sea of shadow. [V, 13] [36]

From a horseman's point of view, which immediately becomes the
reader's, this rising and sinking of houses is what "seems" to be
happening. It is hardly possible to form a closer verbal approximation of a moment of perception, but the mind so quickly adapts
to such an activity that when it is presented as fact rather than
momentary illusion, the result is a shocking sense of strangeness. In
contrast, Crane's use of "seems" or "perhaps" for events normally
taken for granted creates an indefiniteness of statement that he further increases through his penchant for negatives. This style acknowledges the limitations of language and the multifariousness of

"the real thing"; often it is only possible to say what a thing is not, and often it is necessary to state that a thing is only "perhaps" what it appears to be. As a narrative strategy, such prose, then, becomes a prose of implication, marked by silences; its essential subject always borders on the inexpressible. Crane is exploiting the natural reticences of American speech, but his use of them is consistent with his interest in the transmission of unstated thoughts and feelings, as when two men look at each other in "a curious silent communication" (VI, 298). At such moments, it seems that Crane, his characters, and his audience come together as "modern" men, working within an essentially isolated and solipsistic predicament. Hesitant expressions of what might be known about experience really become flirtations with those laws and dynamics of experience which, as Crane says, "no man may give tongue to" (VI, 136).

The information given by Crane's prose is therefore severely limited. There is an understandable absence of what Erich Auerbach has called an absolute Flaubertian "faith in the truth of language." [37] For Crane, experience must be transformed, and in the process language itself is transformed. The particular interpretive procedures which govern those choices of metaphor, simile, and point of view that are responsible for the evocation of Crane's strangely imagined world will be discussed in another chapter. A few conclusions, however, can be drawn from this primarily descriptive study of his style, showing how thoroughly certain attitudes and conceptions invest all his work, even the shaping of sentences and phrases. Considered only in terms of language and syntax, Crane's style is one which interprets life as fragmented and unpredictable, something about which it is difficult to form express conclusions. It attempts to render immediacy through presentation of sensible data before that data has been integrated and perhaps falsified by reflection. An insistent use of the passive voice shows man to be as much acted upon as acting, for experience is interrelational; a man brings as much to an event as it brings to him. The surface quality of life, colors, textures, odors, and sounds, bombards man's senses and influences response; but perception is not absolutely distinct from projection. Beneath mannered or formally stiff phrasing lies the assumption that even to begin approaching the truth of experience, one must present more than one point of view, occasionally within a single sentence.[38] But Crane maintains a guise of objectivity even when he projects emotional responses or interpretations into a scene that the reader is made to think he sees with his own eyes: "The loud soldier blew a thoughtful cloud of smoke from his pipe" (*RB*, 213). A "picture" is drawn, and the smoke is emphasized because it is from perception of the manner in which the soldier smokes his pipe that an on-the-spot observer deduces his state of mind. Frequent use of emotions as agents of action ("Amazement instantly smote him in his tracks"; VIII, 266), shows how emotional states can overwhelm personality, flood consciousness, qualify perception, or, again, elicit an action ("He had blindly been led by quaint emotions"; VI, 53). Fragmentation of syntax reflects a chaotic movement of man's thoughts matching the immediate chaos of events. Finally, Crane's prose shows that the essential quality of immediate experience is that it is beyond absolute control or understanding, despite the shape and order which may be imposed upon it through language and reflection. His problem then was to find individual, immediate, and intense incidents that magnified habits of human perception, sensation, and emotional response, incidents which, to borrow his phrases, were of "the fabric of dreams" (V, 66) and of the "unreal real" (V, 49).

❧ 2 ❧

CRANE'S HABIT OF
IMAGINATION

———•—•———

> *. . . life as seen through a pair of strange,*
> *oblique, temporary spectacles.*
> A LOVELY JAG IN A CROWDED CAR

Stephen Crane is often compared with Ernest Hemingway, and the most extreme of the many comparisons is Daniel Hoffman's claim: Hemingway's "view of reality is essentially the same as Crane's." [1] Despite several similarities between the two writers, one important way they differ seems more enlightening than all the links between them. To borrow Johnson's riposte about Swift, it might be said about Hemingway, with only a little qualification, that the rogue never hazards a metaphor. Crane is just the opposite. At their most extreme, Crane's scenes seem not so much observed reality as reality metamorphosed. In his fiction, a mournful stream may look at men with white eyes. Tents may spring into strange plants, and campfires may become peculiar red blossoms. This is more than impressionism; it is transformation. If Hemingway's idea of the "real thing" is "the sequence of motion and fact which made the emotion," [2] then Crane's is often the sequence of motion and fact as seen through "a pair of strange, oblique, temporary spectacles" (VIII, 364).

"There is at the back of every artist's mind," Chesterton wrote, "something like a pattern or a type of architecture."

> The original quality of any man of imagination is imagery. It is a
> thing like the landscape of his dreams; the sort of world he would
> like to make or in which he would wish to wander; the strange flora
> and fauna of his own secret planet; the sort of thing he likes to think
> about. This general atmosphere, and pattern or structure of growth,
> governs all his creations, however varied.[3]

Crane supposedly told Willa Cather that he was able to write *The
Red Badge* speedily because "he had been unconsciously working
the detail of the story out through most of his boyhood."[4] The
statement may not have been Crane's,[5] but its general truth seems
undeniable. Crane's virtual transposition of the landscape of his
imagination into *The Red Badge* produces what A. J. Liebling calls
"the true merit of the book, which is about a boy in a dragon's
wood, and timeless."[6] The repetitive characteristics, tones, images,
associations, and distortions of Crane's scenes and details show the
extraordinary importance he placed on his personal aggregate of
stored emotions and imaginings. His habit of composition confirms
the supreme confidence he had in the rightness of his vision. "The
detail of a thing has to filter through my blood," he told Cather,
"and then it comes out like a native product, but it takes forever."[7]
No wonder Crane felt that in some things an artist was "powerless as a dead snake."[8]

"An Experiment in Misery" offers a particularly apt example of
this transformative imagination.[9] The objective of the young protagonist, as set forth in the story's prologue, is to discover the feelings, "point of view or something near it" of a tramp. An older
friend suggests to him, "You can tell nothing of it unless you are in
that condition yourself." That condition is identified with "Rags
and tatters, you know, a couple of dimes, and hungry, too, if possible." Almost as soon as the boy adopts this condition, references
to objective facts give way to interpretations by a predisposed
imagination. Common everyday objects suddenly become threatening. Cable cars are "dangerful and gloomy, breaking silence only by
the loud fierce cry of the gong"; a station for elevated trains
"seemed to resemble some monstrous kind of crab squatting over
the street." People and things are no longer autonomous in this en-

vironment. Even the tramp's feelings and point of view are abandoned for a different kind of perception:

> The swing doors snapping to and fro like ravenous lips, made gratified smacks as the saloon gorged itself with plump men, eating with astounding and endless appetite, smiling in some indescribable manner as the men came from all directions to a heathenish superstition. [VIII, 284]

Such writing is not primarily descriptive or analytic; all details are unified by a hallucinatory apprehension of scenes, in which objects are threatening, devouring, malignant, and finally demonic. Life in this world is a form of living death. In the flop house "there suddenly came to his nostrils strange and unspeakable odors that assailed him like malignant diseases with wings." The reader is removed from social and historical reality and given entrance into hell:

> To this door came the three men, and as it was again opened the unholy odors rushed out like released fiends. . . .
> There was a gas jet in a distant part of the room that burned a small flickering orange hued flame. It caused vast masses of tumbled shadows in all parts of the place. . . . [VIII, 287]

Spatial and temporal reference vanishes; perspective of a sharp, realistic picture blurs into a grotesque vision of an underworld graveyard intended to generate a particular "strange effect":

> And all through the room could be seen the tawny hues of naked flesh, limbs thrust into the darkness, projecting beyond the cots; upreared knees; arms hanging, long and thin, over the cot edges. For the most part they were statuesque, carven, dead. With the curious lockers standing all about like tombstones, there was a strange effect of a graveyard, where bodies were merely flung. [VIII, 288]

Fiends lurk, and men are either as much as dead or "wildly tossing in fantastic nightmare gestures, accompanied by gutteral cries, grunts, oaths." Vision of this milieu is essentially subjective, for when dawn breaks, "daylight had made the room comparatively commonplace and uninteresting."

The sociological conclusions Crane draws from this experience

are equally commonplace. Forcibly his own is the quality he dis-
cerns in the experience and his single-minded persistence in conveying that quality. All the incidents and scenes of lower life holding special significance for Crane appealed to his emotional
predisposition to perceive the elusive and strange, even the occult
and demonic quality of experience. Such was the habit of his imagination that even in "An Experiment in Luxury," a sketch emphasizing the uninteresting life of a millionaire and his family, a transformation occurs. Crane's persona finds himself "a wanderer in a fairy
land. . . . He was an invader with a shamed face, a man who had
come to steal certain colors, forms, impressions that were not his."
Nor were they those of an ordinary, common-sense vision. In this
millionaire's house, amid activities of the most harmless kind, the
reporter is immediately intimidated by the "quick, strange stare" of
a footman who later "moved with a mournful, deeply solemn air."
In this scene of calm domesticity, the visitor notices a "cool abun-
dance of gloom . . . lurking plants." Again there are those colors
that cast a hellish hue through the dungeon of the flop house:

> An immense fireplace was at one end . . . a fire burned redly. . . .
> A softened crimson glowed upon the head and shoulders of a bronze
> swordsman, who perpetually strained in a terrific lunge, his blade
> thrust at random into the shadow, piercing there an unknown some-
> thing. [VIII, 296]

Even before the visiting reporter has entered the house, his transformative imagination is at work. Instead of a concrete pictorial
description he offers only a bizarre perception: "The house was
broad and brown and stolid like the face of a peasant." Like the
saloon, the house is invested with human attributes, but, we are
told, "It had an inanity of expression, an absolute lack of artistic
strength that was in itself powerful because it symbolized something." That "something" is apprehended later when with the same
flash of surrealistic perception, the reporter sees that while watching a kitten, the "man of millions was in a far land where me-
chanics and bricklayers go, a mystic land of little, universal emotions," and that his wife's "features were as lined and creased with
care and worriment as those of an apple woman." It is possible now
to surmise that the footman moves with a "deeply solemn air"

because he, with his "refined" nose, is in many ways less a peasant than are those he serves. Crane's imagination does not stop with this relationship between the people and their house. The house is "a complete negation," but "from another point of view . . . it stood as a fetich, formidable because of traditions of worship." It assumes human characteristics because it eventually becomes more than a fetish, more essential than the people themselves; for the people have relinquished their humanity and are now controlled by their objects of worship. The millionaire's wife has been so compulsive, so obsessive in her scramble "for place before the white altars of social excellence" that she has lost whatever vestiges of sophistication, civilization, indeed humanity she might once have had. She impresses the reporter's excited imagination not as an irritable, discontented, pinched old lady, which is how she would strike one's common sense, but as something transformed: "a savage, a barbarian, a spear woman . . . a Zulu chieftainess . . . a dragon." [10]

If this is symbolism, it is symbolism of a peculiar kind. Normally, through repetition, an image will grow and accumulate a complex of values and feelings until it becomes a symbol. The house in "An Experiment in Luxury," like a symbol, suggests something larger than itself, its literal sense is deformed; but rather than growing in value and feeling, it changes. Crane improvises his associations and plays with meanings; he finds new, particular, ephemeral uses for his "symbols" until what they originally represent, no matter how complex, becomes their least important attribute. They begin to function more like fictional characters than symbols. Also, there is little need to guess what these arbitrary "symbols" originally do stand for, little need to refer to a schematization apart from the story itself. Crane strives to be unmistakable and often provides self-imposed definitions that rarely remain fixed for long. His "symbols" usually point to some inexpressible truth about a particular moment without becoming part of a larger systematic design. For example, the first three paragraphs of section 11 of "The Monster" might be described as confrontation between Judge Hagenthorpe's ivory-topped cane and Henry Johnson's unbandaged eye. But it is not enough to say that the eye, representing irrationality, nonconformity, or individuality has triumphed over the cane, representing rationality, respectability, or social stability. Knowledge of what those objects might represent does not unlock the significance of this silent drama. The cane functions as more than a symbol of judgeship, more than an embellishment, more than a signature of the judge's personality. As Crane explicitly states, the judge is able to think at his best only when he is slowly rubbing the cane's ivory top; but the cane simultaneously serves as a kind of narcotic, for the judge does not express his true thoughts or feelings unless he has mislaid the cane. The reader knows what the judge thinks of the "monster" and assumes that the judge checks his thoughts when confronting Trescott because he has his cane. Yet there is also the restraining force of the Negro's eye. The actual meanings of both the cane and the eye become secondary to their use as devices for suggesting a radically complex psychological portrait and interaction. What appears to be a straight, realistic description accords again with Crane's habit of imaginative deformation. Unseen emotional and psychic forces control this scene. Crane is still wearing those strange spectacles that allow him to pierce through this most placid of scenes and perceive with "the magic of the unwinking eye."

Magic eyes, mystic places, fairy puffballs, fire-imps, bloody specters, sacrificial priests, great ghostly robes, ominous babes, savages, monsters, assassins, fiends, red snakes, East Indians, ghouls, and dragons roam through the landscape of Crane's imagination. They do not appear in all his work, and when they do, they are not always treated seriously; but these nightmare figures do help to define that landscape from which details of experience in Crane's fiction acquire their emotional and "symbolic" import. Crane's imaginative filtration, the overlapping of simple observations with childhood images evoking our deepest feelings of dread, awe, terror, or excitement, has all the properties of a dream that discovers the powerful associations between our truest desires or repulsions and the apparently innocent surfaces of the world we inhabit. These affinities are unavailable to logical investigation and must flash forth as apparitions, hallucinations, bearing all the deformed truth of a fairy tale. A child may disregard such fantasies when he is told monsters are not real, only to discover later that the fairy tale was right, there are monsters in the world; there are labyrinths, ogres, events that evade the orderings of reason and morality.

In "Death and the Child," the correspondent is in tune with what really is happening in battle; the long cartridge belt crossed on his chest clutches him like the arms of the dead soldier it once belonged to, and the rifle taken from another dead man "was as unhumanly horrible as a snake that lives in a tomb." To a veteran's eye they are only a rifle and a cartridge belt, but Peza's hallucination reveals what they really are: a dead man chokes him, and upon his palms he can feel "the movement of the sluggish currents of a serpent's life; it was crawling and frightful." The same imaginative activity governs war stories that are more sparsely drawn. It is present in the near hysteria of the officers in "The Upturned Face," though it is never mentioned. In this story Crane adopts the pose of the realistic observer, and his methods of deformation reveal themselves in his persistent use of tactile and aural images rather than visual ones. Only the upturned face—"chalk-blue"—his "gleaming eyes," and his tunic, "the first button [of which] was brick-red" are seen vividly in the story. This restriction of detailed visual images and the numerous references to voices, touches, the dull beat of the pick, the windy sound of bullets, and the plops of dirt on the body must have been what caused Berryman to feel, "No amount of reading will convince one that it does not occur at night." [11] Crane disproportions the senses by restricting some and stressing others, just as dreams often do, and once again makes a nightmare world. The coming together of the sublime and the grotesque in Crane's fiction generates powerful reverbations, but Crane makes his nod to daily reality by rooting the profound in the commonplace, often the trivial. In "A Mystery of Heroism," Collins runs through a "terrible field over which screamed practical angels of death. . . . The sky was full of fiends who directed all their wild rage at his head"; yet "Collins ran in the manner of a farmer chased out of a dairy by a bull."

Every writer has his prepossessions. They filter through his work, appearing occasionally in concentrated forms that offer clues to his fundamental conceptions. They are often gratuitous. But the recurrent patterns of event haunting Crane's imagination have a special importance in relation to his fiction. He wrote about ship and raft wrecks at least five times before he himself went through that same experience.[12] In some ways, more similarities with "The Open Boat" can be found in an early story, "The Reluctant Voyagers," than in Crane's newspaper account or "Flanagan's Short Filibustering Career," written after the sinking of the *Commodore*. The men in the open boat smoke cigars and ride their bucking bronco, while one of the reluctant voyagers, in a boat that for a moment acted like an animal, wishes that he had a cigar. The rescuer of these castaways is a man with a halo in the first story and a miraculous person in the second. Just as the two men facing the unknown in "Across the Covered Pit" (1892) "clutched each other's hands in the most affectionate manner possible," the reluctant voyagers find their souls bound together, and the men in the open boat experience a "subtle brotherhood." It is a futile question, but one can still wonder how much Crane, the great destroyer of preconceived notions, accurately predicted about such an experience, or how much his prior imaginings gave shape to his own experience in an open boat.

More important than these patterns of event are the images Crane used to give situations his personal stamp. The authority of these images no doubt stems from Crane's uncommon ability to tap those deep memories and feelings that are the roots of personality. Since it was on this activity that he based his habit of composition, it is understandable why he once described an artist as "nothing but a powerful memory." [13] Of all the images Crane drew up to give emotional color to his unearthly world, the most frequent is that of fire.[14] In one form or another it pops into story after story; the most famous instance is, of course, when the flames in "The Monster" break loose as fire-imps and burning flowers. But even in "The Open Boat," when a shark appears, "There was a long, loud swishing astern of the boat, and a gleaming trail of phosphorescence, like blue flame, was furrowed on the black waters."

The earliest extended treatment of fire appeared in a newspaper sketch under the title, "When Every One Is Panic Stricken." The entire sketch is interesting. Unfortunately, it is too often read solely

for the occasion it provides for psychoanalytic speculation about
Crane's concern with rescues, rescuers, victims, and other figures
and patterns of subjective experience that may tenuously suggest
larger mythic patterns. It might be better read simply as a good example of the kind of fiction Crane wrote and the kind of impulses
his imagination was most inclined to follow. The sketch appeared
as a newspaper report in the New York *Press* in 1894. Howells and
Edward Marshall, editor of the *Press*, praised Crane's vivid report-
ing, which, in fact, anticipates most techniques recently claimed as
innovations by practitioners of the so-called new journalism. The
old newspaper questions of who, what, where, and when become
subordinate to the impressions of the journalist himself, who immediately establishes his presence and continues to exist throughout the sketch as its central persona. There are snatches of conversa-
tion, disconnected flashes of observers, a sudden glimpse of "a fire
patrol wagon, as if apparitional," a shifting about in search of small
but human details, and finally a concentrated attempt to make the
reader feel the dread, fear, and excitement as though he were
sweating in the heat from the flames. Like a piece of new journalism, the sketch moves from a factual to a personal account, but
Crane goes further in his subjectivity than any of the new journal-
ists: there is no evidence that the fire ever occurred.[15] This is the
scene as the flames reach their full fury.

> These people of the neighborhood, aroused from their beds, looked
> at the spectacle in a half-dazed fashion at times, as if they were con-
> templating the ravings of a red beast in a cage. The flames grew as if
> fanned by tempests, a sweeping, inexorable appetite of a thing,
> shining, with fierce, pitiless brilliancy, gleaming in the eyes of the
> crowd that were upturned to it in an ecstasy of awe, fear and, too,
> half-barbaric admiration. They felt the human helplessness that
> comes when nature breaks forth in passion, overturning the ob-
> stacles, emerging at a leap from the position of a slave to that of a
> master, a giant. There became audible a humming noise, the buz-
> zing of curious machinery. It was the voices of the demons of the
> flame. The house, in manifest heroic indifference to the fury that
> raged in its entrails, maintained a stolid and impertubable exterior,
> looming black and immovable against the turmoil of crimson. [VIII,
> 340–41]

In this sketch Crane becomes what Michael Arlen calls the new journalist, "less a journalist than an impresario." [16] Stephen Crane presents, The Great Bakery Fire! The fire itself is the center of attention, and like the orange flame in "An Experiment of Misery," it casts a hellish hue. [17] More than that, the sketch appears fallaciously to attribute voices to the flames and to invest them with wills of their own. The thematic purpose of this moment, however, is actually opposed to anthropomorphic conceptions; instead it emphasizes the energies in events that are beyond man's control and unavailable to his normal vision. The entire event becomes occasion for describing the fearful astonishment that the observers experience when they find themselves powerless before the energies, the demons, that normally lurk unseen in the world. Since this is the true, if disguised, nature of things, man's situation is pathetic, and such moments can provide a distancing commentary on that pathos. Crane is explicit about this function in "A Man and Some Others":

> Finally, when the great moon climbed the heavens and cast its ghastly radiance upon the bushes, it made a new and more brilliant crimson of the camp-fire, where the flames capered merrily through its mesquit branches, filling the silence with the fire chorus, an ancient melody which surely bears a message of the inconsequence of individual tragedy—a message that is in the boom of the sea, the sliver of the wind through the grass-blades, the silken clash of hemlock boughs. [V, 60]

Human fate is so inconsequential in the bakery fire sketch that Crane forgets about a baby left in the burning house, as well as a policeman who had run in for an attempted rescue. Only the flames matter, burning with a "terrible hue of red, the color of satanic wrath" amidst the "looming black" of the house. In story after story Crane uses this colorful contrast of fire flashing out of a looming darkness. But here the contrasting colors also indicate the seemingly incompatible emotions arising from an apprehension of the contrasting qualities of the event. The transformative moment spotlights the gloomy, threatening aspects of experience and their induced responses of fear, dread, and revulsion; but the event is also splendid. The observers are attracted to the fire and look at it in an "ecstasy . . . of half-barbaric admiration." Combinations of attrac-

tion and repulsion, the grotesque and the sublime, satanic wrath
and visionary ecstasy, all reflect the dual impulse of Crane's imagination.

To speak of Crane's "double vision" is almost to indulge in a critical cliché.[18] It is apparent in the frequent vacillation of his point of
view between immediate engagement and indifferent withdrawal.
His characters are presented as both pretentious and scared, Berryman remarked,[19] and Crane is both at war with his characters and
on their side. The problem with most discussions about Crane's
"double vision" is their emphasis upon the deflationary, negative,
or ironic aspect of his imagination. It is true that Crane saw himself
primarily as an iconoclast. He seems to have been born with that
divided consciousness upon which ironic vision necessarily depends. It is also true that the main thrusts of his irony are directed
at his characters' pretensions; but Crane's irony is of a special kind.
Even in his earliest known story, "Uncle Jake and the Bell-Handle,"
written when he was fourteen, the ironic high point of the sketch is
not, as has been said, that an old farmer "almost brought out the
fire engine by pulling on a bell-handle which he didn't recognize as
one." [20] Rather, as Jake pulls on a bell handle, "it came to pass that,
at precisely that moment, a waiter of the hotel made a terrific onslaught on a [dinner] gong that was sure to make any horses in the
vicinity run away and awaken all the late sleepers for blocks
around," and Jake excitedly announces to his niece that *he* has
"called out the fire department, or the police force or the ambulance
corps or something else that's awful." The irony is that Uncle Jake
thinks he has caused an event of major importance and terrible consequence. Chance or fate contributes significantly, but of more importance are the character's misperceptions of the situation, or (ex-
panding the theme) of himself and reality in general. Crane's irony
does not always stop at this point. The misperception can produce
actions so influential to a situation that the false perception becomes a true one. The Swede's role in the events of "The Blue
Hotel" is a good example. Another typical situation in many stories
is that a great proposal (no matter how ideal, honorable, or normally valid) is necessarily ineffectual. In these situations there are
usually two aspects of dramatic irony at work. First, things are not

what they seem to be; real situations (whether in the West, or in the Bowery, or in war) never quite match our preconceptions of them. Second, man proposes but God (or Something) disposes; expectations never seem to find fulfillment in actuality. Even obstacles imagined to be mountains, once overcome, appear to be paper peaks. The discovery made in many stories is that of Little Nell in "God Rest Ye, Merry Gentlemen": "Like many preconceived moments, it refused to be supreme."

Crane's irony was pervasive; he directed it at his characters, his readers, his friends, and himself. In following Emerson's directive to congratulate yourself if you have done something strange in a decorous age (VIII, 315), he facetiously assumed Billy-the-Kid and Bowery-tough poses for the likes of Ford Madox Ford and Henry James.[21] Always eager to shock, Crane wrote poetry and fiction that were shocking in their destruction of idols, but perhaps more shocking in their tendency to create them. Simultaneous with every impulse to reduce, diminish, and deflate is the impulse to enlarge, intensify, and even idealize. Thus the bakery fire. But even on a simpler level, there are those personal sympathies and loyalties that consistently appear and sometimes betray the more serious concerns of his art. He admired gallant men and gallant animals, but a more boyish conception of courage seems to subvert the profounder investigations of *The Red Badge*. He detested any form of cowardice and criticized Bowery jays for "a lack of ambition" and a tendency "to willingly be knocked flat and accept the licking" (*Letters*, p. 133). His understandable admiration for men who had been over the rim of combat and who could go back strongly influenced his later war stories—often, though, to the detriment of his earlier insights into the horrors that codes of honor block from view. In short, Crane's dual sensibility was not unlike that of the spy in "This Majestic Lie":

> Somewhere in him there was a sentimental tenderness, but it was like a light seen afar at night; it came, went, appeared again in a new place, flickered, flared, went out, left you in a void and angry. And if his sentimental tenderness was a light, the darkness in which it puzzled you was his irony of soul. This irony was directed first at himself; then at you; then at the nation and the flag; then at God. It

was a midnight in which you searched for the little elusive, ashamed spark of tender sentiment. Sometimes you thought this was all pretext, the manner and the way of fear of the wit of others; sometimes you thought he was a hardened savage; usually you did not think but waited in the cheerful certainty that in time the little flare of light would appear in the gloom. [VI, 206]

While many preconceived moments may not be supreme, the opposite may occur; a trivial or unheroic moment may unexpectedly blaze with sublimity, as the Kid in "The Five White Mice" discovers when, faced with death, he experiences the "unreal real," the scent of hay, or perhaps the memory of that scent. "It had no right to be supreme but it was supreme." There always remains in Crane a desire to rescue something from the shambles left by his irony, as in this description of a tattered division of soldiers in "War Memories":

There wasn't a high heroic face among them. They were all men intent on business. That was all. It may seem to you that I am trying to make everything a squalor. That would be wrong. I feel that things were often sublime. But they were *differently* sublime. They were not of our shallow and preposterous fictions. [VI, 249]

Perhaps Crane suspected that his own description of the sublime would slump into a shallow fiction, or perhaps such a description was not what he would call his "trump," [22] or perhaps he knew that any statement about soldiers' virtues would be dull and reductive. At any rate, at the end of "War Memories," Crane's feeling that there was something ineffably radiant about a bedraggled group of soldiers drives him to tell the reader, "The episode was closed. And you can depend upon it that I have told you nothing at all, nothing at all, nothing at all."

This positive strain of Crane's imagination—the impulse to project light into the gloom—often permits metaphor or simile to overwhelm the literal characteristics of an observed detail. The most extreme instances of these disembodied images are found in the poems, where there is often no frame of reference by which even to begin an interpretation. As Berryman says, "They are perfectly self-possessed," [23] and any relationship to reality as it is commonly accepted must be forged by the reader. The acknowledged surrealism of Crane's poetry makes Ruth Miller's tabulations and statistics showing the poetry's scarcity of metaphor and "burnished image" somewhat misleading,[24] for mere frequency of some literary device is no guarantee of artistic effect. For example:

> In the desert
> I saw a creature, naked, bestial,
> Who, squatting upon the ground,
> Held his heart in his hands,
> And ate of it.
> I said: "Is it good, friend?"
> "It is bitter—bitter," he answered;
> "But I like it
> Because it is bitter,
> And because it is my heart."   [BR, 3]

Certainly the description of the first five lines contains no metaphors besides the central one, and the words that outline the scene do not compose striking independent images (desert, creature, heart, naked, bestial), but in the combination a shocking image is formed.

Warner Berthoff has formulated one of the more useful ways of distinguishing the kinds of poetry Crane wrote: "There are those that make assertions, and there are those (or passages in them) that compose incontrovertible images." The poems, he says, "come to life as they manage to convey the sense of some self-contained and irreversible apprehension; otherwise they offer remarks." [25] Miller speaks of the event in "Once there came a man / Who said" (BR, 5) as "an apparition," and it is as apparitions that Crane's poems effect their peculiar if limited appeal.

> On the horizon the peaks assembled;
> And as I looked,
> The march of the mountains began.
> As they marched, they sang:
> "Aye! We come! We come!"   [BR, 37]

If this poem "means" anything beyond itself, it is impossible to say exactly what, but as in the bakery fire, we can be certain that from the point of view of the observer, something both dreadful and splendid is happening. A simple "We come. We come." would threaten and induce fear, but the *singing* of "Aye! We come!" is no doubt awesome. A similarly intense apparitional moment dominates "A row of thick pillars," though the mood is different:

> A row of thick pillars
> Consciously bracing for the weight
> Of a vanished roof
> The bronze light of sunset strikes through them,
> And over a floor made for slow rites.
> There is no sound of singing
> But, aloft, a great and terrible bird
> Is watching a cur, beaten and cut,
> That crawls to the cool shadows of the pillars
> To die.   *[PPP, 125]*

The poem suggests significance, but unlike Yeats's vision of a rough beast slouching toward Bethlehem, Crane's poem offers no framework, Christian or otherwise, in which the "row of thick pillars," the "cur," and the "great and terrible bird" can produce specific reverberations beyond themselves.[26]

Such self-contained images and scenes present special critical problems in the context of Crane's fiction. Usually they are not so extremely independent as those of the poems, but at times they begin to assert their own autonomy: "one could see across [the river] the red, eyelike gleam of hostile camp-fires set in the low brows of distant hills" (*RB*, 201). In the next chapter of *The Red Badge*, no connection at all is made to the literal fires or hills; only the eyes are seen: "Staring once at the red eyes across the river, he conceived them to be growing larger, as the orbs of a row of dragons advancing" (*RB*, 210).[27] One might argue that in the fiction Crane contextually establishes an ironic discrepancy between what a character sees and what the reader comprehends. Those "red eyes" are not indicative of Crane's manner of observation, an argument might go; they are the character's hallucinations, and Crane's objective narrator would reveal them as such. All the dragons and monsters in *The Red Badge* present Henry's falsifying vision; such a "narrowing and deluding point of view" is always juxtaposed with "the enlarging and ruthlessly revealing point of view of the observer-narrator."[28]

The contrast between a character's delusions and Crane's "ruthlessly revealing" vision is present in some stories, particularly the early Sullivan County tales. But as Crane's fictional perspective became more complex, contrasting points of view began to produce subtle relations and effects that refuse to fit rigid schemes of true and false. To Crane truth was pluralistic, and he depended upon multiple points of view and paradoxical configurations to present its complexity. At the same time that parodic aspects mock and devalue sentimental attitudes, the story may actually enliven sentiments that have gone dead in their repetitive stock forms—as in "The Open Boat." Dividing Crane's point of view produces an either-or schematization that makes his work critically manageable and opens it to paraphrase. But language, too, is technique. Transformative moments, though they may seem delusive, have a place, project a tone, produce a texture, bear a weight as part of the total imaginative impression of the book. The "red eyes" depend upon Henry's excited state of mind for their existence, but it is that state of mind, its whirlings, confusions, hesitations, that supplies the interest of the first two-thirds of the novel and also justifies Crane's use of a bright palette to evoke the terrors and ominous brilliance of war as it strikes a tender sensibility. Such a sensibility is necessary for adequate perception of the dragons among events. Beside the tedium and grossness of war, Crane wanted to convey a vision of something awesome and dazzling—and war through Henry's eyes provided that opportunity.

Delineation of two opposing points of view perpetuates an illusion that the organizing principle of a story or novel has been grasped, when in fact the interaction of points of view is simply the author's technique of discovering and presenting new aspects of experience. At times apparitional flashes are the only means of revealing the quality of an event, that ineffable quality normally unobtainable by analytic thinking; it may be apprehended but not fully comprehended. Yet the "vision" itself may be qualified by a "realistic" perspective. Meanings accumulate; no single image or point of view is sufficient in itself, but in combination they can suggest an unstated point of balance where "meaning" might be intuited. For this reason one must avoid the tendency to view Crane's fiction in the same way as that curious kind of story which closes a series of bizarre events with the admission that the foregoing was all a dream. The disclosure apparently justifies a dismissal of all that has happened. Yet the dream itself is still the story, and though the last line can explain the story's rationale, it can neither explain nor justify the reader's experience of the story itself. Crane's fiction calls for a "both-and" rather than an "either-or" approach. The revelation in "An Experiment in Misery" that "daylight had made the room comparatively commonplace and uninteresting" does not invalidate the grotesque "truths" experienced during the night. When those visions do happen to be delusions, like "the pearl-hued joys of life as seen through a pair of strange, oblique, temporary spectacles" (VIII, 364), Crane may mock them; but it is important to recall that the visions seen through similar spectacles constitute a major portion of his work. Even when illusory they have to be accepted as part of reality—the way a mind works and its tendency to play tricks on itself. Only in the abstract can they be dismissed from the stories; in context, they form an integral part of the reader's experience. Crane was often in sympathy with such a vision,[29] for it reflects a life of the imagination which he, as an artist, indulged. Besides "pearl-hued joys," such a vision can give access to truths unavailable to common modes of perception and understanding:

> "I have heard the sunset song of the birches
> A white melody in the silence
> I have seen a quarrel of the pines.
> At nightfall
> The little grasses have rushed by me
> With the wind men.
> These things have I lived," quoth the maniac,
> "Possessing only eyes and ear.
> But you—
> You don green spectacles before you look at roses."   [WK, 82]

Crane's vision of the world is strange enough to be called maniacal, and in terms of ordinary perception, it is as though he had donned spectacles; but from his point of view the reverse is true. What may appear false from one point of view may have its own validity in another realm of experience—the psychological, for example. Or as in the poem above, the speaker can say, "These things have I lived," because in moments of intuitive transport his experience became one with that of nature.

Crane was aware of the discomfort caused by trapping the reader between two incommensurable perceptions that qualify each other without canceling each other out. In "Coney Island's Failing Days," a stranger is bothered when he dines by the sea because, as he says, " a man with a really artistic dining sense always feels important as a duke when he is indulging in his favorite pastime," yet at the same time the sea always makes him feel like a trivial object. "The conflict of the two perceptions disturbs me." It is not always easy to resist the temptation to simplify conflicts of perception in Crane by registering a preference for one or the other. The tendency to stress the narrator's "true" vision as opposed to a character's "false" vision too often produces a kind of critical commentary that reduces his work to a treatise on how men *should* perceive, think, and act rather than accepting it as a presentation of how men *do* perceive, think, and act.

Crane's earliest stories provide good examples of the transformative imagination in rudimentary form. Even at the beginning of his career when, as he later said, he could hardly think what to write about, he invested his comic episodes with an aura of the ominous and supernatural, characteristics traditionally found in *Blackwood's* fiction and in frontier tall tales, which, according to Constance Rourke, featured a "stress upon the supernatural" and "a distinct bias toward the grotesque, or the macabre." [30] These elements, discernible throughout Crane's career, are clearly visible in his early Sullivan County tales and sketches. Their dramatic situations, like those of most of the poems, can be reduced to some strange adventure or encounter; in the tales they always occur in the woods. Hunters stare into a rock den at "fiery eyeballs," or they tumble through darkness toward "a strong, yellow light." The central protagonist of the tales and the butt of Crane's irony is the "little man," who is always crawling into caves, hollow trees, or openings in a thicket, or approaching mysterious houses, or encountering strange characters at night. The little man's sense of wonder is never a natural response to normal events or to nature's observable characteristics; it is rather a heightened response to events in a few of nature's dark corners. Such a subjective reaction to things, marked by exaggeration, became a staple of Crane's fiction.

Ostensibly these "little grotesque tales of the woods" (*Letters*, p. 59) usually begin as hunting or fishing stories, but their deviations are in keeping with frontier tales. As Rourke points out, the origins of frontier tales probably go "back to fairy tales of Europe in which a hunter or poor man wanders all day without finding game and then encounters magical events in the forest." [31] Along with the mysteries of the woods and the ways of wild animals, Crane's tales display the mockery of frontier humor. Figures such as a "spectral dog," "a mysterious hermit," a "brown giantess," "a white-robed phantom," and a "mesmeric mountain" are exposed as a frightened animal, a goofy farmer, an enraged woman, and other common, usually harmless, people and objects. The cry of the little man, whose stomach is aching from too much huckleberry pudding is heard by his comrades as a "cry of the unknown" whose "tones told of death and fear and unpaid debts," the surreal scream of "a savage [who] saw a burning home" (VIII, 258). Later in his career, in the bakery fire and "The Monster," Crane would provide serious, realistic settings for such cries of the unknown and for the reactions of modern "savages" actually standing before or within a burning home.

The Sullivan County tales are essentially comic, but they are not simply burlesques; while they parody macabre melodramas and tall tales, this comedy itself, like the humor in tall tales, "verged toward that median between terror and laughter which is the grotesque." [32] The ironic deflation of the little man and his "swelling emotions" consistently saves these tales from the purely ludicrous; yet there is often a discrepancy between evocation of mood and ironic wit. In "Killing His Bear," Crane bombards the reader's senses. The hunter can feel his nerves tingling and hear his blood surge, throb, swim, and curdle in his veins. Green pines huddle and sing together. The stillness is gray and ponderous, except for the baying of the hound. Despite the parodic force of these descriptions, in the context of the tale they acquire too much emotional weight to be dismissed as literary ridicule, or as merely the excesses of the character. Something else is at stake which the tale's irony is too feeble to deny. There is some seriousness of evocation in the following passage, an attempt to remain true to the hunter's immediate experience:

> Slowly the little man changed his aim until it rested where the head of the approaching shadowy mass must be. It was a wee motion, made with steady nerves and a soundless swaying of the rifle barrel; but the bear heard, or saw, and knew. The animal whirled swiftly and started in a new direction with an amazing burst of speed. Its side was toward the little man now. His rifle barrel was searching swiftly over the dark shape. Under the fore-shoulder was the place. A chance to pierce the heart, sever an artery or pass through the lungs. The little man saw swirling fur over his gun barrel. The earth faded to nothing. Only space and the game, the aim and the hunter. Mad emotions, powerful to rock worlds, hurled through the little man, but did not shake his tiniest nerve.
>
> When the rifle cracked it shook his soul to a profound depth. Creation rocked and the bear stumbled. [VIII, 251]

The language may seem extreme—"Creation rocked"—but even laconic Hemingway made the earth move when his Robert Jordan was with Maria, and Crane is describing the culmination of this hunt as a sexual moment. "The earth faded to nothing": the man's personality, Crane might have said, faded to nothing. After his experience,

> The little man yelled again and sprang forward, waving his hat as if he were leading the cheering of thousands. He ran up and kicked the ribs of the bear. Upon his face was the smile of the successful lover.

The little man is once more himself, a frivolous soul, like a lover who, in gloating over a conquest, forgets the steeps of passion, forgets that his soul was shaken to a "profound depth."

Irony is never absent. Even during the climactic moment of this conquest, one might remember Crane's article, "Sullivan County Bears": "Contrary to general belief, the shyest of all the animals which naturally live in these woods is the bear, and not the deer." Consequently, a bear hunt is a diminished thing. (Crane's sympathies are clear. Several of his early *Tribune* articles deal specifically with wild animals, and though some propose to honor legendary feats of hunting and tracking, Crane always sides with the animals.)

These deflations of the bear hunt still do not negate the little man's immediate experience, although one can be sure that *after* the experience he will be its worst interpreter, just as are the men in "The Last Panther," who "cheered and went home and told about the killing of the panther." In a later sketch, "The Snake," a man kills a rattler. " 'Well, Rover,' said the man, turning to his dog with a grin of victory, 'we'll carry Mr. Snake home to show the girls.' " After the adventure the man functions normally; his victory speech will certainly not include how he became a different person while in battle with the snake and "went sheer raving mad from the emotions of his forefathers and from his own." In "Killing His Bear," Crane is on the edge of letting two realms of experience coexist in uneasy balance, and he is on the edge of letting a subjective response maintain its splendor despite contradictory prosaic facts and after-the-fact emotions which are deflationary.

In some ways the ironic situation of this story seems merely an excuse for Crane's creation of a splendid imaginative moment.[33] Similarly, the ironic discrepancy between delusive imaginings and objective facts is only a thematic framework for an earlier story, "The King's Favor" (1891). A South African king, an honorable warrior held in British captivity, is able to transcend his actual circumstances and imagine himself again as a great warrior. The stimulus for this illusion is a song by a visiting American tenor. The chief's fantasy is delusive, and its terms are extravagantly romantic, but the description of his response to "an inspiring war song" stands apart from the cute, mocking prose of the rest of the story, suggesting that if anything about the story seized Crane's own imagination, it was this moment:

> His eye, grown sullen and down-cast from years of captivity, again flashed, and his chest heaved. He was again a great chief, leading his hundreds of brown-bodied warriors, snake-like through the rustling grass to where the red coats and bayonets of the stolid, calm Britons glimmered and shone in the sunlight. He heard the swift rush of hundreds of naked feet, as his warriors swept down on the immovable British square, and writhed and twisted about it like a monstrous serpent. He heard the low muttered war chant of his followers, sounding to his enemies in the distance as the most ominous and dreadful of forebodings; the great wild cry of the battle as his

swarthy demons dyed their spears in the white man's blood; the
yells and curses of the Britons as they went down, blanched and pale
and bloody, to death. He saw the ghastly faces and gory bodies of
his enemies lie thick amongst the brown grass. [VIII, 571]

The implicit assumption of this passage is that art has a certain kind
of power. Just as a war song moves the king, so, too, is nineteen-
year-old Crane trying to move the reader with this unrealistic and
parodic, yet emotionally charged passage (this impulse is also at
work in the description of the bear hunt). In contrast, the prose in
the remainder of the story is flippant. Structurally, the stylistic
labors of the passage are justified, since there is no pretense that
this is a literal description of some historical battle. It is fantasy. But
the paragraph exceeds its function in the story, and becomes not
only a virtuoso display of sparkling word combinations, but also
the exercise of a power, an attempt to evoke and incite emotional
response.

The kinds of response Crane wants from the reader seem to be
those very states of wonder, awe, or transcendence which he habitually attributes to his characters. This activity is again part of the
positive aspect of his imagination. Even when such moments are
presented sentimentally, as when Fleming enters the "religious half
light" of a forest chapel (RB, 235), psychological penetration and
truthfulness govern the presentation as much as ironic intention.
Mostly in times of stress or tension, though not impossibly during
the calmest of times, perception narrows and sense becomes oblivi-
ous to all else except the one thing that seems to generate sudden,
overwhelming significance. The meaning of the object in view is
often incidental to the experience itself, a sense of absolute clarity of
vision. It is a mystical experience in the sense that the electrified
object—whether a house, a shoe, or a field of corn—eludes definition and strikes a newly acquired sensibility as pure significance.
Crane may stress such a moment with a statement like "this blanket, dangling before a hole in an adobe wall was to Richardson a horrible emblem" (V, 18); but he may or may not do much to explicate
the emblem, for the importance of the moment lies in the consciousness of the character. The character reaches a still point, his
sense of self diminishes, and he becomes attuned to the outside

world. He becomes part of that world's unity or chaos, and acts not so much like one who is dreaming but like one who is dreamed. The object of his vision strikes him as immensely clear and precise or as strange and incomprehensible—or both. In either case, his consciousness extends to a point where he himself is lost in the mystery of his apprehension.

The unknown or incomprehensible may be something as simple as not knowing that a "ghoul" in a cave is really a harmless farmer, or it may be an event such as "the mystic process of the closing of the day." In "Mr. Binks' Day Off," Binks and his wife experience such a moment.

> The Binkses had been silent. These songs of the trees awe. They had remained motionless during this ceremony, their eyes fixed upon the mighty and indefinable changes which spoke to them of the final thing—the inevitable end. Their eyes had an impersonal expression. [VIII, 313]

Binks himself can only mutter, " 'I wonder why,' he said; 'I wonder why the dickens it—why it—why—' " Even if he could say, "I wonder why it all has to pass," Binks would not express the depths of a moment which also accentuates the confinement and pettiness of his daily life in the city.

During these moments—whether Crane presents them by stressing the sudden importance of a trivial object or by emphasizing the largeness of the emotion experienced—the character becomes a barbarian in a state of primitive astonishment. It is precisely this state Crane wishes to impose upon the reader—to make him, once again, a barbarian. Crane uses descriptions of barbarism in several ways. The millionaire's wife in "An Experiment in Luxury" is negatively described as a barbarian, a spear woman, a savage; and soldiers who cease to be "men" in the frenzy of battle are described similarly in *The Red Badge* and in Crane's war stories. But a barbarian may also be a person faced with something, no matter how commonplace, that he cannot comprehend and thus stands in awe of, as Crane said of himself in a letter to Nellie Crouse:

> However, you have awed me. Yes, indeed, I am awed. There is something in your face which tells that there are many things which you perfectly understand which perhaps I don't understand at all.

This sounds very vague but it is nevertheless very vague in my mind. I think it means that I am a savage. Of course I am admittedly a savage. I have been known as docile from time to time but only under great social pressure. I am by inclination a wild shaggy barbarian. I know that I am hopelessly befogging my meaning but then at best my meaning is a dim thing. I intend to say at any rate that the light of social experience in your eyes somewhat terrifies this poor outer pagan. [Letters, p. 111]

Scratchy Wilson in "The Bride" becomes this kind of comic barbarian, "a simple child of the earlier plains." When "not at all comprehending" the marshal's marriage, he is "like a creature allowed a glimpse of another world." Usually in Crane's work, that glimpse of another world is the reverse of Scratchy's, and more like that of Mr. Binks or the observers of the bakery fire, a glimpse into what our comfortable, self-protective illusions of the everyday—our self-induced sleep—keep us from seeing.

Seeing need not be identified with understanding. *What* you see is not so important as *how* you see. If a character in Crane sees mountains where there are only paper peaks, he is mocked, as is "a vision that magnifies with microscopic glance any fly-wing of misfortune" (VIII, 493); but, as we have seen, Crane is more concerned with the ability to recognize what lies beyond the commonplace. Ultimately, the artist is the hero of Crane's fiction, a man whose vision is more charged than that of people whose normal view is conditioned by complacency. "As the terrible, the beautiful, the ghastly, pass continually before our eyes we merely remark that they do not seem to be correct in romantic detail" (VIII, 665). While the artist can see the beauty or terror of the ordinary, most people, as Crane realized, unfortunately required (and desired) "some loud painful protestation that would bring the proper thrill to their jaded, world-weary nerves—wires that refused to vibrate for ordinary affairs" (VIII, 382). His tales of violence and adventure are just such stimuli, so charged by his transformative imagination that at their best they function as does a girl's scream in "An Eloquence of Grief":

People pity those who need none, and the guilty sob alone; but innocent or guilty, this girl's scream described such a profound depth of woe—it was so graphic of grief, that it slit with a dagger's sweep

the curtain of common-place, and disclosed the gloom-shrouded
spectre that sat in the young girl's heart so plainly, in so universal a
tone of the mind, that a man heard expressed some far-off midnight
terror of his own thought. [VIII, 383]

Like the girl's scream, Crane's art discloses specters and seeks to
touch the reader's own emotions. Like the scream, his art is also
"graphic." The reader may become like the correspondent in "The
Open Boat," intensely aware of a scene "spread like a picture before
him"; or as in "Three Miraculous Soldiers," there may be "something very theatrical in the sudden appearance of these men to the
eyes of the girl"; or as in "An Ominous Baby," a child may follow
an ordinary carriage "with awe in his face as if contemplating a
pageant." The numerous theatrical similes and metaphors in his
work suggest that Crane's imagination conceived of itself as staging
particular kinds of scenes.[34] But as in graphic arts, the scenes are
frozen; they present processions or pageants as if rendered by
strokes on a two-dimensional surface. "It seems that a man must
not devote himself for a time to attempts at psychological penetration," Crane once wrote. "He can be sure of two things, form and
color" (VIII, 436). In "An Experiment in Misery," he directly refers
to this kind of composition while it occurs: "The people of the
street hurrying hither and thither made a blend of black figures,
changing, yet frieze-like." Often Crane seems to envision his work
as a great piece of cloth into which he weaves outlines of his
scenes.[35] Enemy forces in "The Little Regiment" appear at one
point as a "mighty pageant"; later, as night descends, the details of
an army camp are transformed into the materials of a weaver:

Ultimately the night deepened to the tone of black velvet. The
outlines of the fireless camp were like the faint drawings upon an-
cient tapestry. The glint of a rifle, the shine of a button, might have
been threads of silver and gold sewn upon the fabric of the night.
[VI, 11]

The effect of such a scene is not solely visual; Crane goes on to
admit there "was little presented to the vision," but he knows that
"to a sense more subtle there was discernible in the atmosphere
something like a pulse; a mystic beating." The intention behind
this effect seems to be the one expressed in "War Memories":

> I bring this to you merely as an effect—an effect of mental light and shade, if you like; something done in thought similar to that which the French Impressionists do in color; something meaningless and at the same time overwhelming, crushing, monstrous. [VI, 254]

A particularly firm example of Crane's "mental light and shade" is his sketch, "A Fishing Village." In the simple activities of fishermen and of those who clean the mackerel, Crane can find both the sinister and the splendid. From one point of view he sees the destruction of fish for money and profit as sin; from another, he perceives "the mystery and solemnity of the trade." Despite the sketch's irony and interspersed observations of the trivial, the presentation gradually takes the form of a visionary procession:

> Here twenty people of both sexes and all ages were preparing the fish for market. The mackerel, beautiful as fire-etched salvers, first were passed to a long table, around which worked as many women as could have elbow room. Each one could clean a fish with two motions of the knife. Then the washers, men who stood over the troughs filled with running water from the brook, soused the fish until the outlet became a sinister element that in an instant changed the brook from a happy thing of gorse and heather of the hills to an evil stream, sullen and reddened. After being washed, the fish were carried to a group of girls with knives, who made the cuts that enabled each fish to flatten out in the manner known of the breakfast table. And after the girls came the men and boys, who rubbed each fish thoroughly with great handfuls of coarse salt, which was whiter than snow, and shone in the daylight from a multitude of gleaming points, diamond-like. . . .
>
> A vast tree hung its branches over the place. The leaves made a shadow that was religious in its effect, as if the spot was a chapel consecrated to labor. There was a hush upon the devotees. The women at the large table worked intently, steadfastly, with bowed heads. [VIII, 494]

The religious hush of this scene brings to mind Amy Lowell's comment about Crane's attitude toward religion: "He disbelieved it and he hated it, but he could not free himself from it." [36] Perhaps his childhood immersion in religion left him with a sense of the miraculous; in any case, it never left him, though he was always open-eyed to life's constant betrayal of religion's traditional wonders. His poems are really sermons, and the bitterest are like sermons written by the devil. Crane's sensibility, though, was finally not religious; he did not see the external world either as a thin veil drawn over the divine or as a vast system of symbols whose significance awaited his discovery. He was more like his hero Henry Fleming, who shook his fist while the opaque sun refused to invest death with any transcendent meaning. Crane's art is an example of a more modern conviction that the meaningful must often be wrenched into existence. Unaltered life, Crane seems to say, relies on an inner vision for whatever significance it acquires. Lewis Hind could not understand why Crane was so overanxious about the right description of a huddle of bananas,[37] but that meticulous patience was his method. Probably those bananas were becoming radiant, just as a dying soldier's skin in a war story turned "pale blue, and glistening, like the inside of a rabbit's skin" (VI, 153). We can almost watch Crane's transforming powers at work in his revision of the opening of "Moonlight on the Snow." The first draft does all that one normally might expect from the initial words of a story. The sentences establish place, time, theme, characters, conflict, suggested resolution, and introduce historical and social forces affecting the concrete situation. But the method is not typically Crane's:

> The citizens of War Post were annoyed and dubious. They had not expected that the first man to fall under the shadow of the new rule against promiscuous shooting would be Ignatius Burke, the talented young bar-keeper, the man who had chiefly concerned himself with the passing of the law. It seems that War Post had been getting a bad name. The word had gone among the mountain trails that when the stranger went to War Post there was hardly a known line of conduct which would please that critical town and the stranger usually came away bewildered and bandaged. Three-ace Frederickson, a well-known brawler from Fargo City once sojourned in War Post and afterward he often cared to tell his impressions. . . .
>
> For a long time War Post had taken a high pride in her sinister fame. . . .
>
> All went well until certain real estate booms began to strike here and there among the hills. New towns leaped into being [V, cxxii–cxxiii]

The opening of the final version of the story lifts the situation into a conflict between devils and angels. War Post becomes momentous; it glows in a strange light:

The town of War Post had an evil name for three hundred miles in every direction. It radiated like the shine from some stupendous light. The citizens of the place had been for years grotesquely proud of their fame as a collection of hard-shooting gentlemen who invariably "got" the men who came up against them. When a citizen went abroad in the land, he said, "I'm f'm War Post." And it was as if he said, "I am the devil himself."

But ultimately it became known to War Post that the serene-browed angel of peace was in the vicinity. The angel was full of projects. . . . [V, 179]

The artist may wander in a world of stillborn symbols, but what he sees and the meaning of what he sees are secondary to a particular way of seeing. The first sentences of "The Little Regiment" describe how the fog gives the coats of an infantry column "a luminous quality . . . a new color, a kind of blue." So, too, "The Palace Hotel at Fort Romper was painted a light blue, a shade that is on the legs of a kind of heron, causing the bird to declare its position against any background." The transformative power of this sentence lies in the word "declare." The word is a product of that artistic sensibility which can invest the visual with the added power of the aural, and the sentence prepares the reader for the screaming and howling of the hotel itself. Also, it gives the bird an authority of its own, as if its declaration were an assertion of its will, the same kind of willful assertion Scully made when he painted the hotel and that Crane himself wills through his art. The ultimate purpose of his art seems to be a creation of a similar artistic sensibility in the reader himself. To capture the reader Crane may have to resort to the shock power his transformative methods have of making something new and strange. The effect depends on an art that stresses immediacy, for the luminous quality of objects is usually only momentary. At the same time, their strangeness forces the reader to contemplate them as if from a distance. Like the artist, the reader becomes both involved and detached. Immediacy is also required where the creation of this sensibility is slower paced, as in the first paragraph of "An Ominous Baby," in which time must stop while sentence after sentence slowly alters the reader's vision and creates a new angle of perception. One might wonder, at this point, how many of those works of art that continue to survive through generations of readers are less the result of their endorsement of some "universal values" than they are the result of this effort to create slowly in the reader a certain sensibility and framework of perception. The basic assumption of Crane's method is that the most insignificant of objects, even an array of tiny toes jutting from a torn shoe, if properly perceived can become something monstrous, overwhelming, crushing, not in the sense of necessarily providing some new form of knowledge but in offering the senses and consciousness a new fullness and awareness. In such moments the surfaces of inconsequential things take on a new look. All this matters because, as Crane's art finally implies, there is a hint of the divine in such moments of heightened perception and feeling.

It is small wonder that, in the largest sense, art became Crane's idol. Regardless of his themes, his fictions are reflections of situations perceived and felt in this heightened state. Or, if nothing else, they are testimonies to the existence of that intensity. It is unrealistic to portray all of life's moments at such a pitch, and this is one reason why Crane tended toward short fiction and toward intense subjects that matched his habit of imagination. If one were to dig for a message in this particular artistic activity, it could only be that art or artistic sensibility is a bulwark against the surrounding void. As Crane's fiction shows, man's inclination is to give the unknown a name, to call it a vampire or dragon or whatever. Or, as Henry Fleming does when he accepts the codes of his regiment, man may accept social custom as a blinding defense against it—anything at all, just so long as he does not have to confront its pitiless blankness and to experience the dread one knows at the edge of the grave. But Crane knew that the only true bulwark was self-generated: a full use of consciousness, the acceptance and enjoyment of sensation as sensation, the ability to see. A particular state of consciousness, as William Gass says, is the whole of what we are at any one time. "At any time, if it is thrilling, we are thrilled; if it is filled with beauty we are beautiful. It is our only evidence that we live." [38] Crane's art was his evidence that he lived. If Henry Fleming finds any "salvation" at all it is in that moment when he sees with the purity of a mystic, when everything is made clear to him except why he himself is there.[39] Besides perception, there are Fleming's sensations at this time, and Crane captures what Norman Mailer describes as the "curious sensuousness of combat, the soft lift of awe and pleasure that one was moving out onto the rim of the dead." [40] Too much sensitivity in such situations, however, may render a man incapable of functioning as his "duty" demands. In "Death and the Child," Peza's visionary perception causes him to run from the battlefield, while in contrast a fat, greasy, squat soldier stopped munching on a piece of hard bread, "placed it carefully on a bit of paper beside him as he turned to kneel in the trench" (V, 139–40). Although the two modes of perception are equally valid, one of them cannot survive in the world. Yet both can thrive in art. The real hero, the artist, can present the truthful complexity of experience as it registers on the exposed nerves of a recruit and through the "realistic" eyes of a veteran. Each tempers the other, but only the artist can share Peza's vision without succumbing to its limitations.

During this double activity the artist becomes much like the correspondent in "The Open Boat," who looked at the shore and "understood with his eyes each detail of it." In that moment the correspondent loses all sense of self, but this is not the kind of depersonalization which occurs when a pain, a fear, or apprehension so overwhelms consciousness that a person becomes what obsesses him and loses sensibility to all else. Rather, the correspondent's consciousness becomes identical with the scene before him, which is a variation of a creative moment. There are moments when details shine with significance or objects become powerful "symbols," but they are only moments; their significance quickly passes. It is interesting that when Crane was visiting Conrad during a troubled time for both men, the older novelist, to sum up and perhaps break the mood of a long silence, said aloud the famous opening line of "The Open Boat," and Crane looked puzzled, unsure at first of what Conrad was talking about.[41] This was Crane's method, to find the right detail for the immediate moment, choosing it for its momentary expressive value rather than for any universal application. This kind of creative act is as much a matter of assertion as perception. The correspondent in the sea perceives every detail of a shore but that shore "was set before him like a bit of scenery on a stage." Because of his truly disinterested vision, "he was impressed as one who, in a gallery, looks at a scene from Brittany or Holland." Crane, the artist, equally disinterested, goes about making those scenes, pictures, friezes, and tapestries so that the reader may understand them with his own eyes. The words Crane uses to weave these scenes are not Hemingway's, which as Mark Schorer remarks, are perfectly suited to his subject, the exhaustion of value.[42] Crane's words project value, even if that value is only the splendor of some unworldly color and form.

❦ 3 ❦

CRANE'S SENSE OF STORY

*He could feel his dulled mind groping after
the form and color of this incident.*
A MYSTERY OF HEROISM

"Set any short story writer to work on a novel," Seán O'Faoláin
once wrote, "and he will inevitably break it up into episodes." [1]
Crane certainly is no exception. His extreme use of episodic structures periodically elicits the complaint that "his work is a mass of
fragments." [2] Even his stories often are broken into numbered episodes, suggesting that this method of narration least distorted his
conviction that significance of experience resides—if anywhere at
all—in isolated, immediate moments. Just as he eschewed the assumption that language communicates a commonly shared conception of experience, Crane also tended to ignore the novelist's assumption that experience is justly apprehended in terms of
progressively developing and interlocking events; he ignored as
well the fictional premise that there is a strict cause-and-effect relationship between actor and action. For these reasons, with story
and style, Crane is still most easily defined by what H. G. Wells
called his "enormous repudiations." [3] But there is a difference in
effect between Crane's rejection of traditional language and syntax
and his rejection of traditional fictional principles of organization.
While Crane's fragmented style brings the reader closer to the action, seduces him into a role of participant and observer, his episodic narratives seem to deny the reader a framework by which to
organize and judge what he has witnessed.

This interpretive elusiveness is the hallmark of Crane's central vision of reality as something that may be apprehended but never adequately comprehended. In a typical Crane story, the mental warfare between perceptions and conceptions become the subject as well as the method of his work. Confusion can be the result, for Crane's sense of story sometimes betrays him. Still, it is possible to see in this light that the inconclusiveness of some of Crane's work (like "The Blue Hotel") issues not so much from a failure of artistic nerve as from his willingness to accept the complex irreconcilability of contradictory points of view.

Crane's problem, then, was to present a coherent vision of incoherence. "There should be a long logic beneath the story," he wrote, quoting Emerson, "but it should be kept carefully out of sight" (*Letters*, p. 159). This admission of a need for some formal organization perhaps helps to explain why Crane thought "the word episodic . . . as a critical epithet is absolutely and flagrantly worthless." [4] The label might be applied to any sincere, realistic presentation of a series of episodes; but sincerity and journalistic accuracy by themselves are minimal virtues. Crane said, "Zola is a sincere writer," but to the question "is he much good?" Crane had to answer negatively. "He hangs one thing to another and his story goes along but I find him pretty tiresome" (*Letters*, p. 160).

It cannot be denied that Crane's works are episodic in the normal sense of that word, but an etymologically pure interpretation might help to justify his objection to the label. "Episode" originally meant "coming in besides," [5] referring to the dramatic section of Greek tragedy occurring between two choric songs. But as the episodes themselves replaced the songs as the means for presenting the continuous themes or statement of a drama, what were then incidental were the songs themselves, or any other interruptions in the drama. Crane merely extends this reversal of a convention and eliminates almost all narrative generalizations, "bridges," passage work, or anything that might come in besides the selected incidents that supply a work's central subject, theme, and continuity of statement. In giving (or attempting to give) his novels this particular structure, Crane's narrative methods reinforced the illusion produced by his style. With both he pretended to eliminate anything that might intrude upon what the reader was allowed to see with "his own pair of eyes" (*Letters*, p. 110).

Of course, this uncontrived objectivity is itself an illusion. Crane's formal methods of manipulating response have become more discernible in his short stories over the years, perhaps because modern readers have grown accustomed to stories without plot, character, or apparent form. Since the subject of a story may be a single episode, the development may consist of a growth in reader awareness (which may or may not be shared by the characters), rather than a change in personality, action, or relationships. Experience is no longer a stable thing. The reader often views a situation in a modern story as if through an ever-expanding keyhole, or as if a scene were begun in darkness and ended in light. Crane's method of formally raising and then lowering a curtain on a scene in which "nothing had happened" has become an accepted convention of short fiction. But the method of his best novels presents special problems, even for modern readers, faced with all those episodes. It might be mentioned that a possible cause for this difficulty lies in the fact that for a long period a method opposite to Crane's became the major convention of novelistic storytelling. Though Crane's longer works suggest the flux of experience, his actual presentation is elliptical, abrupt, and fragmentary. The methods of Conrad and James, on the other hand, try to duplicate that flux, both stylistically and formally, and to identify forms of experience with contours of thought as projected through selected central intelligences. Crane's belief in man's "weak mental machinery" (*Letters*, p. 110), as we have seen, would not let him give interpretive responsibility to a single point of view for very long. His sudden shifts in perspective adequately reproduce a modern equivocal view of reality; nevertheless, his substitutions for traditional methods of narration did not become the "modern" novelistic conventions of Proust, Woolf, or Joyce.

Crane best summed up his habit of novelistic composition in describing a novel as "a succession of sharply outlined pictures, which pass before the reader like a panorama, leaving each its definite impression." [6] This so aptly describes the general impression and method of Crane's work, as well as the nature of the reality it presents, that it is easy to neglect the counterproposal couched in this definition. For while a panorama may be exhibited a part at a time, or consist of a series of pictures, its main purpose is to present a continuous scene or a large, inclusive picture. It seems that the reader properly experiences Crane's endlessly qualified scenes or strange panoramas when he is in that world but not of it. As we have seen, through immediately rendered impressions, Crane's style draws the reader into a scene, but that same style, through explicit statement or incongruous images or shifts in diction, forces the reader to consider the presented reality from a detached and often contradictory point of view. This same habit applies on a larger scale to Crane's formal organization. Reader involvement is encouraged through apparently uncontrived presentation of a series of episodes, but the panorama they create is subjected to large shifts in emphasis, and the reader is forced to organize his impressions and judge them according to two or more frames of reference. It is therefore futile to concentrate only on what happens in a Crane work. In *The Red Badge,* judgment of an event according to regimental codes might have to be held in mind until that event is judged according to an individual's scheme of values, and the two may conflict. Or evaluation may have to contend with the discrepancy between perception of an event and reflection upon it, each subject to its own limitations. It is almost as if Crane conceived his work in spatial terms, separating components of a continuous scene and arranging them to achieve a kind of imaginative equilibrium, for the sake of revelation rather than explanation. The final episode of "The Blue Hotel," for instance, acts like a strategically placed figure or patch of color in a painting; it changes the compositional nature of the whole. Crane said he wanted to be unmistakable, but his method challenges the reader. Apprehending the organizing principles of a novel such as *Maggie* requires an appreciation of Crane's alterations in those techniques we normally speak of as form, plot, and characterization—altered techniques by which Crane both orders and delivers his themes.

The first thing that can be said about *Maggie*—it cannot be said about everything Crane wrote—is that the novel's succession of events does tell a story, though it is a banal story of a girl's drift toward prostitution and death. In abstract terms the novel's logic is relatively clear. Repulsed by the reality of Bowery life, Maggie is attracted to fantasies which, for her, find some embodiment and support in imitations of culture and refinement. When these fail her, she journeys into deeper levels of the hellish Bowery reality she wishes to avoid. That reality is hell in three stages: the physical and emotional reality of the tenement and factory, the hell of nonidentity she experiences as a social outcast, and finally suicide. The story as such derives heavily from popular stereotypes, but it offered Crane something his earlier stories never had—an ostensibly realistic subject of apparent social importance in which to exercise his sense of the possibilities of art. What is immediately compelling about *Maggie* is not the social commentary but the intensity with which the novel forces the reader to see and feel before it asks him to judge. *Maggie* is first of all a showpiece, in which the tinsel gaieties and the terrors of slum life display Crane's attraction to the city as spectacle. New York around the turn of the century gave him and many others (for instance, John Sloan, Theodore Dreiser, and James Weldon Johnson, all, like Crane, born in 1871) an intoxicating panorama of city life. Along with several dozen New York stories and sketches, *Maggie* reflects the sense of exhilaration with which all these artists greeted and depicted—at least initially—the city streets, where life, as John Sloan saw it, was "drab, shabby, happy, sad, and human." [7] In *Maggie,* the "yellow glare, that lit for a moment the waters lapping oilily against timbers" formally contrasts with the kaleidoscopic turnings in the wet streets where "Electric lights, whirring softly, shed a blurred radiance." [8] As in all his work, Crane's prose seeks to arouse and excite sensations, not just describe them. In *Maggie* the style is much like the Goncourt brothers' development of *le style artiste,* a style that Charles Rosen describes as designed not to make the reader "understand, but to feel—quite literally to share the sensations of disgust, fear, and desire of the characters of the novel." [9]

Such a style, of course, provides a basis for real "understanding" of life in the Bowery. Crane moves with typical persistence toward immediate points of view and at times describes events only through his characters' perceptions: "He saw two hands thrust down and take [the pennies]. Directly the same hands let down the filled pail and he left" (p. 24). Crane also stresses how Bowery inhabitants emotionally apprehend their surroundings, which to them are neither neutral nor stationary: "The building quivered and creaked from the weight of humanity stamping about in its bowels" (pp. 12–13). By contrast, the mention of "a passive tugboat" and "ignorant stables" intensifies the volatility of the novel's opening scene; while the objective or distancing perspective is provided by the misplaced adjectives, "passive" and "ignorant," which serve here also as interpretive clues to the people who inhabit this indifferent environment. At times the "observer" is placed in the ironic position of viewing a highly charged scene with such total detachment that actors and actions are reduced to abstractions: "The group of urchins burst instantly asunder and its individual fragments were spread in a wide, respectable half circle about the point of interest" (p. 74).

Crane does drive the reader hard with his rapid fluctuations between involved and detached points of view, each qualifying the other; [10] but his writing is most effective, and its irony richest, when he presents both simultaneously, creating an ambivalent perspective that most successfully shocks the reader out of his accustomed mode of perception. The close of chapter 3 shows two terrified children looking at their mother lying in a drunken heap on the floor. A description of "the woman" would be naturally objective and free of false sentiment; a description of "their mother" would be more immediate and perhaps cause sympathetic identification with the children. Crane does both, appearing objective while ironically commenting on a subjective relationship and its departure from an ideal: the children "crouched until the ghost-mists of dawn appeared at the window, drawing close to the panes, and looking in at the prostrate, heaving body of *the mother*" (p. 30; emphasis added).

It is commonly agreed that Crane's techniques are not always under control in *Maggie;* the effect is often strained, and the irony is heavy-handed. What still holds attention in a book that is really little more than a line drawing is its intensity. To hold this story together Crane had to resort to almost a shorthand notation. The simple story line is skillfully reinforced by the step-by-step or scene-by-scene portrayal of the other characters on parallel paths of accelerating degeneracy.[11] There is not even a chance for redemption in *Maggie*. Along with the characters, even their haunts grow seedier, as seen in the increasing shabbiness and vulgarity of the dance halls Pete and Maggie visit. But unlike *The Red Badge*, in which events are for the most part compressed into two days, *Maggie* does spread its action over an extended time period, making it more like a proper novel but producing the problem of maintaining continuity.[12] As a result, lives are defined in old-fashioned, conventional ways, though with extraordinary condensation: "When Jimmie was a little boy he began to be arrested. Before he reached a great age, he had a fair record" (p. 39). References to passing time link chapters together: "Three weeks had passed since the girl left home" (pp. 117–18). To make connections between episodes, Crane at times draws attention to the work as a written record and breaks the illusion that it is an uncontrived, objective presentation of reality: "Upon a wet evening, several months after the last chapter" (p.143). And references to the baby's and the father's deaths are milestones by which experience normally is divided and measured.

An explicit time sequence may be all that is necessary for events to coalesce into a story, but it is not enough to make a novel. The "why?" between events is left out. Why does Maggie become a prostitute? Why does she drown herself? Too often in discussions of Crane's work the idea of plot is discarded without any description of what replaces it. Yet *Maggie* does have a plot, or at least vestiges of one, if plot is understood in E. M. Forster's sense as "a narrative of events, the emphasis falling on causality." [13] Since Crane refuses to be explicit about causality, the sequential narrative of events at first seems to reinforce the attitude that Maggie's fate is simply in the nature of things.[14] Her famous walk to the river in chapter 13 becomes a telescoped version of the downfall of almost any "painted cohort of the streets." The apparently disconnected episodes at the end and beginning, respectively, of chapters 8 and 9 are logically related as question and implied answer. At the end of chapter 8, "She wondered if the culture and refinement she had seen imitated, perhaps grotesquely by the heroine on the stage, could be acquired by a girl who lived in a tenement house and worked in a shirt factory" (p. 73). Chapter 9 opens with an ostensibly objective scene; a drunken woman thrown out of a saloon (the reader does not know she is Maggie's mother) curses the owner and is mocked by a group of urchins. This condition is implied to be the probable fate of many tenement girls, just as the natural fate of many tenement boys is implied in the first chapter as the camera's eye shifts from the battlers in Rum Alley to a shot of "a worm of yellow convicts [who] came from the shadow of a grey ominous building and crawled slowly along the river's bank" (p. 5). The virtual absence of names in the opening and closing three chapters and the reference to characters by epithets ("the forlorn woman") diminish the particularity of their lives and careers.

From this point of view, Maggie's suicide might be attributed to a strictly naturalistic causality, or it may be seen as merely a generic convention. According to the crusading tradition from which Crane probably drew his banal story, a "painted cohort of the streets" has only two escape routes. Both are pictured by the Reverend Thomas de Witt Talmage in *Night Sides of City Life:*

> What way out has one of these fallen souls but the sewing girl's garret, dingy, cold, hunger-blasted. But you say, "Is there no other way for her to escape?" Oh, yes. Another way is the street that leads to East River, at midnight, the end of the city dock, the moon shining down on the water making it look so smooth she wonders if it is deep enough. It is. No boatman near enough to hear the plunge.[15]

So Maggie goes to the river. She is surely a victim of her environment, but only partially. Crane gives a human dimension to her drama; she is also the victim of her own misconceptions about culture and refinement, and the victim of the phony morality of those around her. Crane emphasizes the last cause of Maggie's fate through repetition, parallelism, and contrast. Rejection scenes follow one another in quick succession. Jimmie rejects Hattie; he, his mother, and Pete reject Maggie; and Pete is finally rejected by Nell. "Where kin I go?" Maggie asks, but her path is pointed out to her. "Oh, go teh hell," Jimmie snarls to Hattie. "Oh, go teh hell!" Pete cries out to Maggie. "Maggie went away" (pp. 130, 140). Her death, then, is not just a convention of naturalism or of crusading pamphlets; nor does it go against the logic of the novel, as some have claimed, that Maggie would want to commit suicide after she had become a well-dressed whore.[16] By eliminating a return to the factory as even a possible consideration, Crane emphasizes that whether Maggie leaps or not, she is already dead. As a social outcast, she is a cipher, and her "dream gardens" can no longer support her. Immediately after her seduction she is shown stripped of all independence and owned by Pete who presses "her arm with an air of reassuring proprietorship" (p. 106). Her brother confirms what she has lost. "Well, now, yer a hell of a t'ing, ain' yeh?" (p. 133). She is identified by others as a thing, a prostitute, before she becomes one; but she need not even fill the role, for she already dwells in that modern hell where no sense of self exists. Standing on the street she asks aloud, "Who?" and a passerby unwittingly tells her who she is: "Eh? What? Who? Nobody!" (p. 140).

The whole work is encased, like a parody, in popular attitudes and depends on a reader's own capacity to sort these attitudes out; but he must be guided by the framework Crane provides to evaluate these attitudes. This same framework is the means by which the novel's events can transcend their specific situation and refer to a general scheme of experience. Certainly if *Maggie* is to retain the shock value it once had, it must do more than show that environment is a tremendous thing, or that people in the Bowery are moral cowards, or that a girl can blossom in a mud puddle, or that Maggie's error is to live by fantasies. The pattern emerging from *Maggie* is important not just for the unity it might give the work, but because it provides frames of reference whose contradictions implicate the reader and cause him to question his own conceptions of morality and culture.

Efforts to describe the structure of *Maggie* have usually done little more than make the novel less episodic than it appears to be. Thus *Maggie* has been called a "three-act drama with an appended conclusion"; and it has been quite differently divided into "four major 'perspectives.'" [17] Once when Crane was writing about social form, he said that "form really is truth," and he added that it is "simplicity" (*Letters*, p. 115). A similar simplicity is evident when

Maggie is seen as falling not into three or four parts, but simply into two.[18] It might be worthwhile to think momentarily of the novel conceived in the shape of a reclining hourglass. It opens with a black vision of the savagery, sordidness, desperation, and terror that characterize life in and around Rum Alley. These qualities, presented in the first three chapters in terms of a gruesome fairy tale, inform life in the major institutions of this realm, the tenement, the factory, and the bar. In contrast to this environment are Maggie's vague fantasies of love, serenity, freedom, and power—which she identifies with money, clothes, and the society of Pete, her "knight." From a broad, expressionistic panorama of Rum Alley the novel spirals in toward its middle chapter as Pete and Maggie move toward each other. In chapter 10 they become offstage lovers, and we see the first reactions to her "fall." The novel spirals out again as Pete and Maggie move apart. The novel closes with another broad, scenic presentation, this time of the conceptualizations, rationalizations, moralisms, and false expectations with which society disguises and perpetuates the conditions of existence presented in the opening chapters.

The ironic relation between the chaos of the first chapters and the after-the-fact assertions of the last is Crane's essential subject. The emphasis of the first half is upon the terrible physical and emotional realities of slum life. The narrator keeps his distance; explicit moral concerns are absent. All the furniture broken in *Maggie* is broken in the first half of the novel; and with the exception of the barroom brawl in chapter 11, all the seemingly incessant slaps, slugs, scratches, and kicks occur before the middle chapter.

In the second half of the book the emphasis is upon the moral orderings people use to boost their egos and assert their social positions. Hints of an operative social code appear in an early chapter when Jimmie's father shouts, "Leave yer sister alone on the street" (p. 14), but not until the second half is the idea of "respectability" introduced directly and repeated, as often as five times in chapter 16. In the second half Maggie's mother has stopped using physical destruction to vent her rage against the universe and instead turns it into moralist invectives against Maggie; and "Of course Jimmie publicly damned his sister that he might appear on a higher social plane" (p. 115).[19] This moral posturing is matched by the "cultural" deceptions of the dance halls in which Maggie appears in the second half as a changed person; she is now realistic about "Pete's strong protecting fists" (p. 106). He is no longer a knight who will lead her to "elegance and soft palms," but only a safeguard against her falling back into the grotesque world of the novel's first half. These two general perspectives of the Bowery are not simply to be seen as moral appearance, on the one hand, juxtaposed against an amoral reality on the other. The two are really aspects of the same thing. The moral and cultural attitudes are part of that vicious reality and they are partly the reason for its continuing existence. This is why the exposure of Pete, Jimmie, and Maggie's mother as cowards, liars, and fools is less interesting than Crane's complex depiction of the manner in which self-interest motivates moral passion, and the manner in which the confused linkage of self-interest with social status produces unsocial actions in the name of virtue.

Lurking inchoately in *Maggie* is the formal organization Crane would perfect in "The Blue Hotel." Maggie's sin and death are indeed "the result of a collaboration" (V, 170), but who will accept responsibility? Like the cowboy, each Bowery character implicitly cries, "Well, I didn't do anythin', did I?" (V, 170). Yet blame for Maggie's fate cannot be placed on the other characters alone. If she were only in her world and not of it, as she is initially presented, Crane might have used her as a catalyst—as he later used Henry Johnson in "The Monster"—and based the structure of the whole novel around the polarities of society and hell. Such an arrangement allows a monster and fire to rip apart the social artificialities that screen the chaos society does not want to see, let alone touch. But Maggie is not just a catalyst. Like the Swede in "The Blue Hotel," she ironically collaborates in her own fate, and both characters are in the sway of romantic notions. By the end of the novel, then, the reader is caught in the position of realizing that it is as absurd to forgive Maggie as it is to damn her. Her only transgression is against moral and social codes that are in themselves transgressions of moral and social reality. Yet Maggie shares these codes with other characters whom the reader would never forgive. Like them, she is a victim of self-deception; and like them, she adopts moral poses so as to appear on a higher social plane. Her errors are so perfectly those of her society that forgiveness of Maggie should be extended to others. The forgiving reader is caught in a moral contradiction, or like Maggie's mother, becomes bound to noble sentiments that are in themselves self-serving deceptions.

Denied a normal response to events and characters, the reader is also refused the comfort of those values that he may most deeply cherish. The episodic method itself shocks and upsets normal order through its lack of transitions and its use of juxtaposition, which Roger Shattuck describes as a "great diversity employed to suggest and delimit a point in another dimension." [20] *Maggie* likewise takes its comment into another dimension, for the reader comes to see that the real thing is as unreal as its Bowery imitations. There are theaters, for instance, "giving to the Bowery public the phantasies of the aristocratic theatre-going public, at reduced rates" (p. 60), but the second half of the novel indicates that Crane's ironic attack is actually directed toward the "aristocratic theatre-going public" itself. The "soft palms," "smiles of serenity," money, and "adornments of person"—all that Maggie desires—are no guarantee of love or the serentiy they seem to promise. They are merely the outer trappings of a life based on illusion. The Bowery people are much like their counterparts in a more sophisticated society. A minister, representative of that society, rejects Maggie for the same reasons as do Pete and her family; and the theater-going crowd of New York emerges from a performance with their "hearts still kindling from the glowings of the stage" (p. 144), just as Maggie once did (p. 63, p. 72). When Maggie becomes a successful whore she has a "handsome cloak" and "well-shod feet," and she daintily lifts her skirts as do those women in the crowd who "shrugged impatient shoulders in their warm cloaks and stopped to arrange their skirts". (p. 143). All Crane's indictments of the society crowd's values are implicit except for one sentence in which he directly comments on the illusory basis of their lives: "An atmosphere of pleasure and prosperity seemed to hang over the throng, born, perhaps of good clothes and two hours in a place of forgetfulness" (p. 144). Maggie is familiar with Bowery places of forgetfulness; the most that good clothes and a cloak can give her are additional illusions. Through a series of juxtapositions Crane thus directs his final comment toward that society from which Maggie draws her fantasies and from which the Bowery adopts its moral and social codes. The reader is presumably a member of this society, whose culture, like the Bowery theater and the mission, must be seen for what it really is. Ortega y Gasset bluntly describes the nature of such ideals:

> Justice and truth, too, all work of the spirit, are mirages produced on matter. Culture—the ideal side of things—tries to set itself up as a separate and self-sufficient world to which we can transfer our hearts. This is an illusion, and only looked upon as an illusion, only considered as a mirage on earth, does culture take its proper place.[21]

Although *Maggie* does not have the weight and force of some of Crane's other investigations of conventional values, it does sketch a basic conflict between reality perceived as chaos and reality conceived in terms of certain moral and cultural orderings. Crane will suggest later with greater force that though such orderings may be illusionary, they still may be necessary—if only for survival. As a well-dressed whore, Maggie acquires the manners and adornments of the socially successful; she lacks only status. The rest of the novel shows status to be as hollow as clothes or manners, and those who do have it are not that much different from Maggie, but they are accepted by their peers. They do not go to the river. If rules or communal conceptions are not accepted, then there is no way out except through isolation or death.

Crane may have shared his basic story with the Reverend Thomas de Witt Talmage, yet what must have first shocked readers of the 1890s was not that *Maggie* attacked cherished values but that it totally lacked the condescension with which crusaders of the times approached such characters. Crane was to present for the first time this lower class of society from a seriously rendered, insider's point of view. This perspective is most successfully achieved in the first half of the novel; in the second half, however, when the characters parody middle-class terminology and moral postures to excess, at times they become hybrids who represent neither class realistically. And in his effort to evoke the sensations of slum life, Crane often lets his prose attempt to stimulate more response than the situations themselves seem to warrant. The violence and terror of the first half become repetitious and extreme. It is true that *Maggie* gave Crane a shadowy realistic framework which his earlier stories and sketches never had. He was writing in an accepted and popular genre, but as with the Sullivan County tales, he still pumped more feeling into events than the novel's dramatic structure could support.

With *The Red Badge*, Crane left to others the further puncturing of social ideals sketched in *Maggie*. Turning his attention to the values and rituals of another kind of society, he began probing the hidden and often disturbing nuances of those ideals called heroism and courage. But in comparing Crane's slum novel to *The Red Badge*, we might recall Flaubert's caution that one is not at all free to write this or that. The secret of a masterpiece lies in the concordance between the subject and the temperament of the author. With *The Red Badge*, Crane found a home for his style. He could ask about men in battle, "I wonder how they feel," and let his prose excite extreme sensations for extreme situations, and he could let the exaggerated expressionistic warfare of *Maggie* finally become an objective condition of existence.

Some of the decisions of organization discernible in *The Red Badge* are firmer than those in *Maggie* and move closer to ways in which short stories are controlled.[22] Crane decided to restrict his points of view to Fleming and Fleming's regiment; there *is* a narrative voice but it is that of a disinterested observer whose scope of observation ranges between these points of view. He translates the men's apparent or probable thought and emotions, reports what they do and sense (or seem to do and sense), and for the most part lets the reader evaluate these reports in terms of the circumstances in which they occur. In every way he pretends to disguise his presence. The events themselves, the important ones, occur during two intense days. As in *Maggie*, private fantasies, emotions, calculations, and codes influence the narrative's developing action; but in *The Red Badge*, private experience more frequently becomes the narrative action itself.

At first glance, the novel's general pattern seems pressed from the same die as that of *Maggie*, falling roughly into two halves, each a counterpart of the other. A study of fear and cowardice is juxtaposed against a study of courage and heroism. In the first half, the enemy charges twice. During the second charge, the potential hero views the attacking men as "machines of steel," and he scampers from the battle; he sees those who remain as either some "wondrous breed" or "methodical idiots" and "fools." At the end of chapter 12, and the end of the first day, a soldier leads him back to the camp: "Well, there's where your reg'ment is. An' now, goodbye, ol' boy, good luck t'yeh" (p. 255). The second half begins as a comrade accepts him back into camp; the youth sleeps and the next day again faces battle, becoming one of those he thought to be "machines of steel," not only as a member but as a leader. Again there are two charges. This time, during the second charge, it is the enemy, or most of the enemy, who flees. In the eyes of the regiment and its officers, the boy becomes a "war devil," a "wild cat," a "jim hickey," a "good man."

Focusing upon the central character eliminates much of the diffusion caused by the narrative sweep of *Maggie*. This concentration also allows Crane to take a more daring journey than he did with his girl of the streets, whom he leaves gazing into oily black waters. Like Maggie, Fleming breaks from the social unit that can give him identity, and Crane takes him as deep as possible into that dark pit on whose rim the "moving box of tradition and law" may let him totter. It is as though the narrator has stepped off the bridge in *Maggie* and dared to discover what man builds walls against knowing—that by stripping himself, his society, and the world to its ultimate core, he, like Henry Fleming, must stand in uneasy oneness with what turns out to be nothing more than a cipher, a blank-eyed corpse. Backing away, eventually turning, Fleming soon "began to run in the direction of the battle . . . an ironical thing for him"; but he is "an invader" in that landscape "owned by the dead men," and he must return to the land of the living or become a cipher himself.

In the second half of the novel, the recruit now swings out in a direction opposite from that of the previous day, a direction that again takes him toward death but along a different route. Moving within a community of men, he enters a realm of experience upon which that community imposes significance through its codes and rules. Previously, in the wilderness, Henry had "received a subtle suggestion to touch the corpse." He did not. A summary account of the second half of the novel, in terms of Henry's frame of reference, tells the reader, "He had been to touch the great death, and found that, after all, it was but the great death" (p. 298). Two different views, two experiences of death inform the antithetical halves of the novel, but neither is more true than the other, for both are real aspects of the same thing.

In its formal neatness, the novel's division seems an advance over *Maggie*; the two halves seem as closely related as sides of a coin. On the face of it a hero or coward need be identified only by comparison with his opposite. But in a form where the halves balance as well as contrast, there is another and more disturbing implication. When Fleming runs from battle, he displays "the zeal of an insane sprinter in his purpose" (p. 231), and when he charges, he also looks "to be an insane soldier" (p. 277). As an insane soldier, is Fleming a "man of traditional courage" or "a fool"? "What remains in the mind of the reader," Jean Cazemajou properly points out, "is a series of confused movements with from time to time, 'men drop[ping] here and there like bundles' and, in the protagonist's 'procession of memory,' sad nerve-racking images suddenly blurred with a sense of relief when the 'sultry nightmare [is] in the past.' " [23] This description attests to the brilliance of Crane's depiction of the experience of war, but how is one to judge that experience? The interpretive elusiveness that marks so much of Crane's work is here complicated by the final admission that Fleming feels not only relief but "a quiet manhood." Is this "series of confused movements" meant to coalesce into a dramatic progression toward moral maturation? Or is Crane mocking his hero? Attempts to locate Crane's point of view have concentrated on trying to sort out the statements of the last chapter, but there has been little agreement as to whether Crane was confused, serious, ironic, or ambivalent in his final assertions.[24] Given the narrator's normal reticence, it seems necessary to view these discursive statements in light of the novel's total structure in order to avoid imposing one's own conceptions on Fleming's experience. It is just possible that the idea of a full growth into manhood may be our conventional euphemistic way of thinking about something that never takes place.[25]

In terms of the novel's largest patterns of action, the particular battleground covered, gained, or lost is important only in relation to its effect on the men. Donald Pizer has noticed, however, that this movement provides the novel with a "dynamic structural element independent of plot." [26] In its simplest outline, the novel describes a large-scale advance toward battle, creating suspense, and a final departure from battle, providing a sense of resolution. Within the novel this basic movement is repeated on a smaller scale through a series of advances and retreats.[27] Structurally, war becomes the kind of action Henry himself sees it to be: "wild and desperate rushes of men perpetually backward and forward in riotous surges" (p. 290). Thematically, this structural element of the novel reinforces the view that these movements are meaningless in themselves. The final departure from battle emphasizes this theme, as the men leave the ground they have just fought so hard to gain. Among those who survive, winners win nothing, losers lose nothing; only the "mental attitude" [28] of the men matters.

The structure of the action thus creates a framework within which no ultimate judgments can have much significance. Experience must be evaluated in more limited terms, and Crane provides two frames of reference, Henry's and the regiment's. A regiment judges its members according to what they do. In the confusion of battle, Henry's cowardice goes unnoticed, but his "bravery" is observed and duly acknowledged. Henry shares the regiment's assessment when "he saw that he was good. He recalled with a thrill of joy the respectful comments of his fellows upon his conduct" (p. 297); but he thinks differently when he is actually engaged in events. The form of the novel would seem to suggest that a distinction must be made between Henry's adventures and those occasions—they occur only three times, at the beginning, middle, and end of the novel— when Henry is with his regiment and has time to think during a moment of relative peace.[29] An important distinction is made between a mind's "accustomed course of thought" and "its battleful ways" (p. 297), and there is little similarity between the two. We are made to mistrust the moments when men anticipate events or give them an after-the-fact shape or evaluation. *The Red Badge* explodes Henry's preconceptions and severely judges the reflections of the first day by placing them in an unmistakably ironic context.

At the beginning of the novel, none of Henry's ceaseless calculations bring him satisfaction in his attempt to understand war, nature, or himself; but experience gradually begins to strip away his fantasies. The great movements he thought he would see are replaced by months of monotonous camp life. Expecting "much glory" in war, he is surprised to discover that before battle a horseman is concerned about a box of cigars; in battle, a lieutenant, shot in the hand, swears no differently than if he "had hit his fingers with a tack hammer at home"; and a general observes a battle like a "business man whose market is swinging up and down" (p. 232). This boy, who typically projects his tortured American soul across the sky, finds it "surprising that Nature had gone tranquilly on with her golden process in the midst of so much devilment" (p. 228). Nature provides none of the ultimate answers he is seeking, she offers him only a corpse; and when Conklin dies, the recruit shakes his fist in outrage and frustration. The boy does apparently learn something, but only apparently, for when he rejoins his regiment safely after his desertion, it seems that none of the revelations of nature's indifference have registered. He can still ask, "how could they kill him who is the chosen of the gods and doomed to greatness?" He also reflects that "he had performed his mistakes in the dark, so he was still a man" (p. 264).

During the second day Fleming resumes his battleful ways, and the normal concept of courage is given a rude jolt, for many of his actions and thoughts are as self-pitying and self-seeking as when he was a coward. One of Henry's general expectations, though, does become true, "that a man became another thing in a battle" (p. 219), but not in the way the boy expects. Instead, a man becomes "a barbarian, a beast" (p. 272), "shrieking mad calls and appeals" (p. 293). During the battle madness, Henry experiences a delirium, "a temporary but sublime absence of selfishness" (p. 278); he was "not conscious that he was erect upon his feet" (p. 271), or that there were "words coming unconsciously from him in grotesque exclamations. He did not know that he breathed; that the flag hung over him, so absorbed was he" (p. 291); "dazed and stupid" (p. 278), a man proceeds "sheeplike" (p. 226), driven by an officer so that he moves "mechanically, dully, with animal-like eyes upon the officer" (p. 226). If he happened to lunge into battle of his own will, his motivations were not the noble ones he expected or later asserts; "in a dream . . . he lost sense of everything but his hate" (p. 271), which might be directed at his rifle or at a fellow officer. After battle these "tortured savages" (p. 280) "were men" (p. 284).

At the end of the novel Fleming is certainly a "man" in the sense that he is no longer a savage beast, but his idea of being a man seems grander than his just being human again. He wishes a resolution to the problem he presented himself early in the novel: "He wished to return to camp, knowing that this affair was a blue demonstration; or else to go into a battle and discover that he had been a fool in his doubts, and was, in truth, a man of traditional courage" (p. 219). It would seem to follow that Fleming's final reflections and judgments about himself, many of which bear a pointed resemblance in phrasing to those occurring after his desertion, are no more valid than any other products of his reflection; after all, he bases his estimations on "gilded edges of memory" (p. 297). He may be a man of courage, but that man is certainly not the traditional one of his reflections. Crane most characteristically pursues these dilemmas, not in "The Veteran," so often read as a coda to The Red Badge, but in stories like "A Mystery of Heroism," in which the hero, though "sure of very little . . . had blindly been led by quaint emotions and laid himself under an obligation to walk squarely up to the face of death" (VI, 53). Crane, too, like his character, is sure of very little, but he unflinchingly examines the enigma of a hero who is also a fool.

To say that Henry accurately summarizes and interprets his experience would deny a major premise of the novel, the gap between the mind's battleful ways and its "usual machines of reflection." Fleming's memories are naturally gilded, because what a soldier can truly recall is at most "bits of color that in the flurry had stamped themselves unawares upon his engaged senses" (p. 286). But for

Crane to treat Henry with total irony would deny what the novel so clearly demonstrates: he does become a veteran of sorts, his public deeds are worthy of honor, and during the course of events, his eyes do open to some new ways. What Crane actually intended in his closing remarks is unknowable, but as Merleau-Ponty said somewhat facetiously, "The sum of the accidents of a novel appears as the author's intention." [30] Several of the deletions from the manuscript version indicate that a possible intention was to reduce the irony of the final chapter,[31] but the irony is not totally eliminated. Henry's mind was surely "undergoing a subtle change." He could criticize his acts, but only with "some correctness," and he had defeated "certain" sympathies. During his adventures there was a moment when "New eyes were given to him. And the most startling thing was to learn suddenly that he was very insignificant" (p. 275). However, the proud and bombastic assertions of the last chapter show that Henry considers himself at that moment as anything but insignificant.[32] Though he does seem to show some moral maturity when he realizes he deserted the tattered soldier, Fleming, unlike Wilson or the cheery soldier, nowhere demonstrates that generosity toward others which apparently comes to one who can "perceive himself as a very wee thing" (p. 261). Henry looks back on a romantic figure of himself (a figure that in some ways he had actually become). The final comment on Henry's view of himself is the image of the sun breaking through a cloud. This image is not inherently positive, for in the last chapter of *Maggie* the "inevitable sunlight came streaming in at the windows" to mock Mrs. Johnson. Just as the ray of sunlight appears amid leaden rain clouds, Henry's smile and visions of tranquil skies appear amid a "procession of weary soldiers . . . despondent and muttering, marching with churning effort in a trough of liquid brown mud" (p. 299). Despite Henry's thirst for a soft and eternal peace, the procession, as one soldier suggests, may be "goin' down here aways, swing aroun', an' come in behint 'em" (p. 298). At best the ending is ambivalent. Crane does not deny that Fleming has changed (or that he momentarily feels as he does), but Crane refuses to confirm that the assessment of that change is accurate or permanent.

Henry's least debatable change is a substantial, if not complete, change in mental attitude from that of a recruit to that of a veteran. The perceptions of each are vehicles for revealing two irreconcilable but equally valid ways of apprehending reality. Both as a recruit and as a veteran, Fleming is granted perceptions of almost visionary power. These moments are not open to investigation by usual machines of reflection, since unlike those of the last chapter, they occur when Henry's senses are totally engaged and his normal ways of thinking are suspended. They are also moments of stillness that stand apart from the confusions of a mind's battleful ways. Both scenes strike Henry's extended consciousness with a revelatory fullness and coherence of detail. The first occurs when Henry confronts the corpse in the forest chapel:

> Near the threshold he stopped, horror-stricken at the sight of a thing.
> He was being looked at by a dead man who was seated with his back against a columnlike tree. The corpse was dressed in a uniform that once had been blue, but was now faded to a melancholy shade of green. The eyes, staring at the youth, had changed to the dull hue to be seen on the side of a dead fish. The mouth was open. Its red had changed to an appalling yellow. Over the gray skin of the face ran little ants. One was trundling some sort of a bundle along the upper lip.
> The youth gave a shriek as he confronted the thing. He was for moments turned to stone before it. He remained staring into the liquid-looking eyes. [RB, 235]

Like the corpse, Henry is isolated from his regiment, and at that moment he bears little relation to anything at all, least of all the universe. Stripped of all ties with the living, Henry is reduced to himself; the only meaning and comfort left him is to be found in death. In looking fully at man's plight, Henry reaches the end points of thought and life.

Luckier than Maggie, though, Fleming is accepted back into a society, and as the recruit adopts the "creed of soldiers"; he begins to mimic what he considers to be the ways of veterans. He decides he "had license to be pompous and veteranlike" because no one knew he had run from battle; he concludes that a "man with a full stomach and the respect of his fellows had no business to scold about anything that he might think to be wrong in the ways of the universe, or even with the ways of society" (p. 264). A veteran is a man who simply does his job. Like the cheerful soldier, he may "chuckle with glee and self-satisfaction" or engage in "cheerful and audacious whistling" (p. 255), but he is also a man whose imagination must be kept in rein, whose sensitivity must be depressed, and who, in order to function, must overlook some of the more terrifying conditions in which he finds himself.[33] Like Jim Conklin, he accepts "new environment and circumstance with great coolness, eating from his haversack at every opportunity" (p. 220). In his bakery-fire sketch, Crane elaborates upon the "mental attitude" with which some veteran fireman confront a fire:

> They all, in fact, seemed to look at fires with the calm, unexcited vision of veterans. It was only the populace with their new nerves, it seemed who could feel the thrill and dash of these attacks, these furious charges made in the dead of night, at high noon, at any time, upon the common enemy, the loosened flame. [VIII, 344]

Henry is most like a veteran when he comes to think of "bullets only as things that could prevent him from reaching the place of his endeavor" (p. 293). But even as a veteran, when Henry "was unconsciously in advance" of the charging troops and his eyes had the "lurid glare" of an "insane soldier," he suddenly apprehends the scene before him with visionary intensity. No longer does the landscape threaten him with "tragedies—hidden, mysterious, solemn" (p. 217); rather, through his new eyes,

> There was an effect like a revelation in the new appearance of the landscape. . . .
> It seemed to the youth that he saw everything. Each blade of the green grass was bold and clear. He thought that he was aware of every change in the thin, transparent vapor that floated idly in sheets. The brown or gray trunks of the trees showed each roughness of their surfaces. And the men of the regiment, with their starting eyes and sweating faces, running madly, or falling, as if thrown headlong, to queer, heaped-up corpses—all were comprehended. His mind took a mechanical but firm impression, so that afterward everything was pictured and explained to him, save why he himself was there. [RB, 277]

There simply is no ultimate answer to the question "why?" except the non-answer Fleming confronted in the forest. As when he

faced the corpse, Henry again sees clearly and in detail, and at neither time does he face "an onslaught of redoubtable dragons" or the
"approach of a red and green monster" (p. 230). The second vision
is obviously limited, and yet Henry is then aware of as much as
possible without being overwhelmed by the terrors innocently
masked by that picture. He is in the world but not of it. Accepting
the regiment's point of view, he knows his existence and actions
can have value—according to the creed of soldiers.

The two moments of vision share the same fleeting temporality.
Insights cannot long be sustained in Crane's world, and soon the
outcast Henry is running from attacks produced by his own raw
nerves. Likewise, the moment of "calm, unexcited vision" of the
second half of the book is soon blurred; Henry charges with "his
eyes tightly closed," and his eyesight is "shaken and dazzled." The
two views of the great death cannot be reconciled, synthesized, or
interpreted. For this reason the moral and interpretive frame of reference in the last chapter jars with the perceptual and ironic frame
of Henry's actual experience as that experience is recorded first
through the nerves of a recruit and then through the calm vision of
a veteran.

One might wish the ending of *The Red Badge* were better. It does
miss a chance for major irony, and it runs on a bit too much. But
what Crane does in that couple of pages is not a serious enough
failure to mar the success of the rest. The virtues of *The Red Badge*
are not the formal ones that will be seen in "The Open Boat," and
only a loss of time and energy results from trying to impose a coherence—as if that were the sole criterion of effectiveness—on the
rougher masterpiece. The vitality of *The Red Badge* originated in
Crane's impulse to disregard the novelist's usual view of his work
as an imagined history of events. Reacting to the narrow historic
mentality exhibited in some veterans' accounts of the Civil War, he
said, "I wonder that *some* of these fellows don't tell how they *felt* in
those scraps!" [34] *The Red Badge* shows that they probably do not say
how they felt because they cannot truly remember. One of the reasons the first sixteen chapters of *The Red Badge* are more effective
than the last third of the novel is precisely because they render the
"thrill and dash" of war through the raw nerves of a recruit rather

than through the less excitable perceptions of a veteran. Crane's imagined reproductions of battlefield perceptions and alien states of mind are the real reason the book will outlive other novels whose basis in historical fact may be superior to that of *The Red Badge of Courage*.

The men in "The Open Boat" are like Fleming in that they, too, had been to touch the great death; they, too, "had dwelt in a land of strange, squalling upheavals and had come forth." They too were "fresh from scenes where many . . . usual machines of reflection had been idle" (p. 297); but Crane feels no need to try to interpret their moral experience discursively. It was not his "trump." Instead he presents only the battleful ways of their minds while actually riding in the open boat, and afterwards, when it is assumed a mind could resume its accustomed course of thought, Crane need only say that "they felt that they could then be interpreters."

In "The Open Boat," Crane fixes his attention so closely on immediate experience that the story becomes a step-by-step process of acquiring "new eyes." [35] Everything extraneous to this main concern is eliminated, the question of heroism is not even asked, and Crane moves relentlessly toward unbuffered contact with the realities of existence. "The Open Boat" is then not so much a story of learning as of realization. Certainly the correspondent, who had been taught to be the most cynical of men, knows that nature is indifferent, but hours on the sea cause him to experience this truth with renewed intensity. Though it may be assumed that a growth in awareness affects moral intelligence, the "long logic" of the story is based on a psychological rather than a moral progression. Constant contact with the wind and waves affects, before anything else, the men's senses and perceptions. Gradually, as these unfamiliar circumstances become familiar, natural responses of anger and self-pity give way to general pity and, finally, to no emotion at all. Anxiety reaches its peak when man's mental processes are most active, but fatigue soon drives out rage: the correspondent's mind "was dominated *at this time* by the muscles, and the muscles said they did not care. It merely occurred to him that if he should drown it would be a shame" (emphasis added).

It is the correspondent, the man of words, who discovers that questions based on preconceptions of an event in no way anticipate the questions asked when that event becomes reality. Formulations do not control or explain experience. It is reality itself, the actual immersion in the cold sea, that formulates the surprisingly limited and puzzled realizations of a man in touch with the great death. "I am going to drown? Can it be possible? Can it be possible? Can it be possible?" [36] The correspondent comes as close as is humanly possible to approximating a cosmic point of view when he is both involved in his experience and detached from it. Like Fleming's insights, each of the correspondent's realizations is momentary, occurring only at that time, but unlike Fleming's experience, these series of moments form a progression. That progression may not be truer to life than are Henry's vacillations and regressions, but they do make for a tighter, more compact story and a more decisive impact.

An experience of riding the edge of death is such a mysterious thing that it cannot be reduced to a single meaning. To say only that the men learn of nature's indifference and of their own bonds of brotherhood is to diminish that experience. Multiple points of view are needed to perceive this strange event. The views range from immediate, limited perception—"Far ahead, where coastline, sea, and sky formed their mighty angle, there were little dots which seemed to indicate a city on the shore"—to authorial omniscience: "It is fair to say here that there was not a life saving station within twenty miles in either direction; but the men did not know this fact. . . ." This last remark both provides information and accentuates the point of the dialogue preceding it, the inherent impulse of the human mind to play tricks on itself. Another voice in "The Open Boat" narrates how this experience might perhaps be seen when "Viewed from a balcony." [37] It is a cautious voice, stating only that the men's "eyes must have glinted in strange ways as they gazed steadily astern." The voice often uses a vocabulary (not out of reach of the correspondent) based upon a distant and often sentimental view of such an experience: "It was probably splendid. . . ." It is often the voice of a man safe on the shore jocosely narrating the story: "By the very last star of truth, it is easier to steal eggs from under a hen that it was to change seats in the dingey." These statements serve to remind the reader of an attitude informing the entire narrative; indeed, "Shipwrecks are *apropos* of nothing."

At the same time, in their sentiment and point of view, such statements contrast keenly with the concerns and experience of the men in the boat. They do not contradict the men's experience, but they emphasize its seriousness and intensity. These often light, pithy remarks also give the story some emotional modulation that is not mere contrivance, for despite preconceptions that such an experience at sea is always one of terror, the mood of these statements does not clash with those brief moments in the open boat when tension abates and the men feel a certain "lightheartedness." Also, the voice reflects an emotional detachment which the correspondent himself eventually achieves during the final moments of the story, when he supposedly apprehends his situation properly.

Since the profundity of the men's experience eludes definition, it often can only be measured by reference to what may be considered normal. A series of commonplace objects drawn from life on land—a bathtub, slate, mats, canton-flannel, carpets, prairie chickens, ham sandwiches, a jackknife, eggs, paper, pie, cigars, furniture, tea, a couch, a mattress, a broad fence—are used to help describe this experience. But just as the wind and waves eventually frustrate all attempts to make sense of the situation from a normal, ego-centered point of view, these objects gradually accentuate the gulf between commonplace experience and this grim exposure to sea and sky. By its very nature, this moment on the sea separates elements of experience that are more complexly bound together on land. Both death and life are part of experience on the shore, but on land the reality of death is obscured by social intercourse and human bonds. Its terror is diminished, and man need not constantly face his own limitations. On the sea, only six inches of gunwale separate potential death from a communal existence which is almost a parody of that on land. The men puff big cigars, the cook asks the oiler, "what kind of pie do you like best?" and the correspondent muses about what the experience has taught him and grows to understand "that if he were given another opportunity he would mend his conduct and his words, and be better and brighter during an introduction, or at tea." These actions, words, and thoughts perform two immediate functions: they underscore man's puny position in contrast to the void around him, and they seem to mock those trite pleasures and formalities that dominate life on the shore.

The breakdown of life into the elemental and the trivial performs yet another function: the incongruous juxtaposition creates the story's essential drama, for though the story is certainly about the great death, it is also as much about life. One of the more suggestive remarks about "The Open Boat" is Berryman's comment that "the death is so close that the story is warm." [38] The physical coldness of sea and air, in contrast, makes the cook "almost stovelike" after he "had tied a life-belt around himself in order to get even the warmth which this clumsy cork contrivance could donate." In contrast to the sea, the cold water in the boat is actually "comfortable" when a man settles into it, "huddled close to the cook's life-belt"; and a rower finds that he can "keep his feet partly warm by thrusting them under his companions." There is also "the subtle brotherhood of men . . . and each man felt it warm him." Simple, trivial pleasures and courtesies glow with astonishing warmth. When juxtaposed against cold nothingness, rituals of serving tea or sharing a cigar with friends become things of importance, goods in themselves. If nothing else, they give evidence of life and create human bonds. Only a man who has faced the cruelty and ignorance of the grave, Crane seems to say, can know the true importance of being warm, tender, and kind, even at tea or during an introduction.

To render the actuality of life in an open boat Crane relied on all the sensory and suggestive means that identify his writing at its best.[39] The rowers do not grow tired, but the oars become "leaden"; the men do not move toward land, but "brown mats of seaweed that appeared from time to time . . . informed the men in the boat that it was making progress slowly toward the land." The meaning of "The Open Boat" is the sum of all its details. Yet such details do not make a story. No matter how realistic, a description of four men dangerously adrift on an open sea is still an episode.

Without resort to a traditional plot or conflict between characters, Crane nevertheless instilled this fragment of experience, and many others, with the formal authority of a complete statement. Natural patterns, not *necessarily* dependent on plot development, satisfy man's craving to close every broken circle, to complete every truncated rhythm. For example, the first three chapters of *Maggie* produce an illusion of wholeness not because there is a resolution of conflicting action or emotion but because there is a cyclical completion of natural processes. Events begin in the day, continue into the night, and come to a close with the breaking of dawn. It is a mistake to overlook the formal simplicity of "The Open Boat," for the very simplicity of its organization makes it a more strongly ordered story than if it had been given a carefully contrived plot.

It has always been natural for man to imagine life as a journey, even if the goal of that journey is a biological inevitability. Both things happen at the end of "The Open Boat"; the men reach the real goal of their journey, the comfort of land, and one of the men reaches that end of which any completed journey can be a symbol. The triumph of 'The Open Boat" is that form and theme are one. While the men are on the sea, life and death are fragilely separated by a few inches of gunwale; the men settle into the "cold comfortable sea-water" within the boat, but the correspondent jerks his hand away from the "tumbling, boiling flood of white water" that splashes up from the sea. There are simulations of human comfort in the boat, and there are promises of death from the sea. Comfort is cold while potential death is boiling. Back on the land, order is restored. The comfort that was parodied and the death that was threatened simultaneously became actualities, and the tenuous separation between the two evaporates: at the same time that the "welcome of the land" is "warm and generous" with real blankets, clothes, flasks, and coffee pots, its welcome also consists of "the different and sinister hospitality of the grave."

Reinforcing this simple design is a sequence of events that occur according to a strict but cyclical chronology, beginning with one dawn and drawing to a close with another. Little need be said about the relation of this natural process to the expansion of perception that constitutes most of the narrative "action." Absorbed by the demands of their situation, the men experience a restricted vision, and the first "process of the breaking day was unknown to them"; but after they grow accustomed to life in the boat and less stunned by nature's insult to themselves as individuals, they can begin to direct attention away from themselves and the problems of navigation. As the unfamiliar grows familiar, they are able to look around, and the next dawn is seen both on the water and in the sky. The self-absorbed, questioning, and even raging correspondent becomes a calm, depersonalized observer. His new eyes are more extreme than Fleming's, for he does not even bother to acknowledge that everything is explained to him except why he himself is there. Events have forced him to see with detachment. After a man has been continuously beaten by sea and wind, he becomes a different thing. All the things that once seemed so important to the correspondent now no longer mean that much to him, including his own fate. Not even the actual experience of tumbling into the surf is as he expected, for the "January water was icy, and he reflected immediately that it was colder than he had expected to find it off the coast of Florida. This appeared to his dazed mind as a fact important enough to be noted *at the time*" (emphasis added). No doubt upon later reflection, the correspondent would be surprised at his detachment: the coastline "was very near to him then, but he was impressed as one who in a gallery looks at a scene from Brittany or Holland." Ironically, the correspondent has moved from a state in which he felt such poignancy in the fate of a legendary soldier to one that is nearer to his former schoolboy indifference. Perhaps that soldier's feeling was comparable to his own now that he was tossing about in the water: "when one gets properly wearied, drowning must really be a comfortable arrangement, a cessation of hostilities accompanied by a large degree of relief." This attitude was foreshadowed when, in the boat, the mere passage of time and the increase of fatigue allowed the men to accept their circumstances, to sleep and, as the correspondent does, to look at a shark with the calm, unexcited vision of a veteran. To emphasize the contrast between preconceptions and experience, Crane states discursively,

"The presence of this biding thing did not affect the man with the same horror that it would if he had been a picnicker. He simply looked at the sea dully and swore in an undertone."

When the correspondent is finally flung into the icy water, the reflections, patterns, designs, and poetic sentiments that give point to experience are of little worth. He sees for the first time with his own eyes and trusts his senses. He marvels at things that would never enter the mind of a picnicker who might happen to reflect on the possibility of drowning at sea. His past life does not stream through his mind, he makes no resolutions to mend his ways, he does not ask why he is there, and he is not overcome by frantic impulses to reach safety. "There is a certain immovable quality to a shore, and the correspondent wondered at it amid the confusion of the sea. It seemed also very attractive, . . . and he paddled leisurely." He does not panic or rage when he has "arrived at a place in the sea where travel was beset with difficulty. He did not pause swimming to inquire what manner of current caught him, but there his progress ceased." He sees the shore in its detail, and noticing the captain grasping the leaping boat with one hand, he "marveled that the captain could still hold to it." After awhile, still unable to advance, he does wonder simply, "I am going to drown? Can it be possible? . . . But later a wave perhaps whirled him out of this small deadly current, for he found suddenly that he could again make progress toward the shore."

Amid this limited, uninterpretive rendition of the correspondent's sensations, perceptions, and thoughts, another voice intrudes, that jocular voice of a man safe on shore. A large wave catches the correspondent and flings him safely over the boat and far from harm. This event strikes the correspondent as "an event in gymnastics, and a true miracle of the sea." That other voice adopts a different, ego-dominated point of view and comments that in being tossed by the wave, "the correspondent performed his one little marvel of the voyage." Is this how the correspondent will at times look back on this occurrence when his faculties and his vanity return to him?

After he and his companions have reached the shore safely, when night has fallen and they are probably warming themselves by a fire, "they felt that they could then be interpreters." The statement is cautious; there is no guarantee that they actually can interpret the experience they have had, but they *feel* they can; and that feeling comes only "then," when they are out of the waves.[40] Any discursive statement they might make or any reflection they might have will necessarily be partial and reductive. Crane makes no attempt to sum up this experience, for the total meaning and proper interpretation resides in the "form and color" of the experience itself, for which one must return to the beginning of the story. To conceptualize any more, or to write a newspaper account, would be a false interpretation. As an artifact, "The Open Boat" is already an interpretation, but it is so close a paradigm of the experience itself that anything more would be a distortion.

The dramatic interplay of contrasting voices found in "The Open Boat" is a structural device shared with Crane's poetry. The most obvious example of alternating rhythms and diction is found in "War is Kind" (WK, 76), but there the preferred point of view is clear. More typical are his unexpected presentations of points of view that contradict without cancellation, as in "A man said to the universe" (WK, 96), or "A youth in apparel that glittered" (BR, 27). Like the stories, the poems are usually dramatic units held together by some incremental form and advancing according to a logic that is not immediately apparent. The journey motif of "The Open Boat" appears repeatedly in both *The Black Riders* and *War Is Kind*; however, the use of natural cycles, such as progressive times of day (WK, 93), is a rarity. The "logic" of other poems consists of following a hidden implication to its natural conclusion while apparently developing an opposite statement. Only when the poem is finished does one realize that its ending was implied from the beginning.

> Behold, from the land of the farther suns
> I returned.
> And I was in a reptile-swarming place,
> Peopled, otherwise, with grimaces,
> Shrouded above in black inpenetrableness.
> I shrank, loathing,
> Sick with it.
> And I said to him:
> "What is this?"

> He made answer slowly:
> "Spirit, this is a world;
> This was your home."   *[BR,29]*

The implication of the second line that the man returned "home" is
soon forgotten as what develops seems to be really a description of
some "land of the farther suns" mentioned in the first line. Addition of the word "home" to the second line would show how logically the poem advances; its absence shows how carefully Crane
kept that logic out of sight.

> A slant of sun on dull brown walls
> A forgotten sky of bashful blue.
> Toward God a mighty hymn
> A song of collisions and cries
> Rumbling wheels, hoof-beats, bells,
> Welcomes, farewells, love-calls, final moans,
> Voices of joy, idiocy, warning, despair,
> The unknown appeals of brutes,
> The chanting of flowers
> The screams of cut trees,
> The senseless babble of hens and wise men—
> A cluttered incoherency that says at the stars:
> "O God, save us."   *[WK, 89]*

The opening lines prepare the reader to accept the traditional conception of hymn, and then the poem seems to deviate into a montage of something opposite, but this incoherency is indeed a hymn.
Once again the reader is forced to associate mistakenly the major
notes of the first lines, "slant of sun," "sky," and "blue," to the
subject of the poem (the hymn), ignoring the period and the fact
that this sky is "forgotten" and "bashful," quite remote from the
hymn of the next sentence, which a second look shows to be syntactically linked to what follows rather than precedes it. While omis-
sion of a word can disguise the logic of a poem, an absence of verbs
can make the placement of a period in the midst of incomplete sentences at first seem relatively unimportant.

Just as the opening lines of Crane's poems sometimes are a compression of the drama of the poem as a whole, the famous opening
sentences of "The Open Boat" and "The Bride Comes to Yellow
Sky" are miniature performances of his best short stories. They in-

dicate why his imagination found its truest expression in that genre. The first sentence of "The Bride" fixes the sensation of a train ride through a kinesthetic detail, and that detail also supplies a theme that the rest of the story will develop ("The great Pullman was whirling onward with such dignity of motion that a glance from the window seemed simply to prove that the plains of Texas were pouring eastward"). The limited scope of the short story makes this kind of compression a virtue, and in modern short stories, where normal conventions of maintaining reader interest are drastically reduced, it is almost a generic necessity for statements to engage the reader by conveying information beyond their literal meanings. Details in such charged sentences are never used solely for their pictorial value, as they are in one of Crane's less satisfying tales, "The Veteran": "Out of the low window could be seen three hickory trees placed irregularly in a meadow that was resplendent in spring-time green." This sentence neither propels the reader into the story nor conveys any more information than the words contain. Absent is the wit, irony, and suggestiveness that mark Crane's writing when his imagination is fully engaged, cutting against his own as well as his readers' perceptual and moral assumptions. Ironically, perhaps the sentence does serve an unintentional purpose if it successfully flashes a signal for the reader to approach with caution the assertions which follow. For like its first sentence, this story fails to provoke; it resorts to conventional expression of conventional attitudes in a way that Crane's more alert fiction does not.

Crane was essentially a short story writer because of the kind and amount of information he was willing to provide.[41] In "The Open Boat," he shows little interest in what led up to the situation, either in the sinking of the ship or in the lives of the men who found themselves suddenly flung together; nor at the end does he show much interest in either affirming or denying explicitly that the lives of these men would now be different. Rather, like Collins in "A Mystery of Heroism," he was "groping after the form and color of this incident" (VI, 53). For this reason, a scenic description often conveys a Crane story more accurately than does a thematic description. For instance, are not most of the tensions, ironies, incongruities, and themes of four of Crane's best-known stories implicit in these scenes? Four men smoking cigars in a small boat lost at sea; a man with a shovelful of dirt poised over the face of a dead comrade; an unarmed marshal and his young bride facing a drunken gunfighter in the empty streets of a Western town; a man running with a bucket through a cratered no-man's land. In compressing his imaginative impulses into making such scenes, Crane produced stories that amplify these central tableaux and invest them with emotional color. What is lost in terms of characters and events is replaced by intense rendition of individual incidents. Suggestion replaces direct statement, and depth and penetration are honored over mass and movement. In short, Crane was the most "modern" writer of the American short story in the 1890s. Occasionally he seems to be following Chekhov's advice to cut off the beginning and ending of a story because that is where, according to Chekhov, a writer is most inclined to lie. The opening sentence of "Death and the Child" is a good example of how Crane propels the reader into a story through a sentence that establishes a dominant emotion: "The peasants who were streaming down the mountain trail had in their sharp terror evidently lost their ability to count." A minor piece of information becomes major; it is a typical Crane twist and reminiscent of methods in his poetry. Again, such methods are best suited to the short story. As Seán O'Faoláin said after praising a passage from "The Monster," "A novelist employing so carefully incised an English as this would produce but few books; their movement would be of the slowest; and the effect would probably become intolerable after a time." [42] For this reason, in style, method, and length, even Crane's famous novels are not really novelistic. *Maggie* is not much longer than James's short story, "The Pupil," and *The Red Badge*, as Crane himself said, "is a mere episode in life, an amplification" (*Letters*, p. 79). With *The Red Badge* Crane's attempt to amplify the episode with an imposed novelistic ending is notable chiefly, perhaps, for the difficulties it got him into.

One of Crane's freshest achievements in the short story is his way of giving an episode a sense of completeness without falsifying its ephemeral, inconclusive character. Early in his career, in the Sullivan County tales, he often resorts to endings that presented a soberingly "true" view of some bizarre experience. Even when later stories expressed a more equivocal view of truth, Crane still would often resort to tricky reversal endings, such as the ironic disclosure that a lemon, not the intended orange, has been stolen in "A Great Mistake," or that the bucket of water obtained at great risk in "A Mystery of Heroism" has been carelessly spilled. These ironic endings do not violate the logic of their stories, but even in Crane's time, they were becoming a worn-out convention, and they drew unbalanced emphasis upon themselves as the "point" of their stories. It is more characteristic for the endings of Crane's better stories to seem almost arbitrary, pointless; or if there is a point, its conclusiveness is immediately debatable. As seen with "The Open Boat," it is a mistake to overlook Crane's substitute conventions because of their simplicity. One of the ways—call it a trick—that Crane used to link his limited episode to a large scheme or "meaning" of experience was to end a story with a generalization or moral: " 'War changes many things: but it doesn't change everything, thank God.' " (VI, 47); or, "And this story proves that it is sometimes better to be a private" (VI, 306). The idea is to give the reader the sense that these endings sum up the story; but they are, in fact, pseudosummations intended to begin disintegrating as soon as their immediate formal purpose is achieved, such as the ending of "The Five White Mice," which tells the reader that "Nothing had happened."

Simple completion of an action introduced at the beginning of a story is form enough for a Crane story. " 'What will we do now?' said the adjutant, troubled and excited. 'Bury him,' said Timothy Lean," and "The Upturned Face" ends with the "plop" of dirt that covers the face of the corpse. Nothing can end a story more finally than death, but even then an ending will suggest the continuation of life. "A Man and Some Others" ends with a death, then turns outward to a timeless context, and virtually drops a theater curtain over the scene of the story: "Slowly and warily he moved around it [a corpse], and in a moment the bushes, nodding and whispering, their leaf-faces turned toward the scene behind him, swung and swung again into stillness and the peace of the wilderness." Crane's most common way of ending his stories is simply to have his characters walk away from the scene, a technique that has since become a cliché of the movies: "As the latter began to show signs of beginning pursuit, the little vandal turned and vanished down a dark side street as into a swallowing cavern" ("An Ominous Baby").[43]

All these endings are significant to the history of the short story because they shift the story's traditional emphasis from its conclusion back into the story itself. Each ending, in traditional terms, is inconclusive, suggesting that experience does not come in tidy packages. And yet each ending completes some incremental design, action, or structure and gives the story a sense of finality. The design is the scaffolding for the story's disclosures, and its terminating point usually suggests a transcendent context in which the story acquires meaning, but that meaning is never explicitly defined.

Since Crane's time, readers faced with stories having virtually no plot or conventional action have managed to discover a shift in focal point from the ending to some epiphany or nuance of character within the story. This epiphany may be shared by the character, or it may not, in which case a mask is stripped from the character for the reader's benefit. The form of many of Crane's stories does duplicate this process of growing awareness, and a character's relation to it is often a major motif; but a reading which narrowly interprets stories solely in these terms does not suit Crane's work as well as it might that of Chekhov, Joyce, Mansfield, or even James. First, there are too many other points of view in Crane's fiction, and his characters' insights are usually partial and momentary. Second, in a sense there are no characters in his work, or their importance as individuals is diminished. If plot might be said to issue from interactions between characters, then the sea is as important a character in "The Open Boat" as any of the men. Some of this diminishment of character may be attributed to the genre itself; the short story simply does not allow for characterization as does a novel. One or two evocative details must suffice. The description of Scratchy Wilson's shirt and red-topped boots "with gilded imprints, of the kind beloved in winter by little sledding boys on the hillsides of New England" (V, 117) replaces any number of events which might deflate the character's authenticity as a gunslinger. It might be argued that any fictional character is only a name and a series of words describing gestures and sounds, but it must be admitted that Crane's use of such words is severely restricted. He is even reluctant to name his characters. This apparent lack of interest in creating anything more than a "type" reconfirms the short story as the best genre for this peculiar impetus of Crane's imagination.[44]

Certainly Crane's conception of character is not that of most novelists; it is not even that of most short story writers. Speculation about the peculiar anonymity of Crane's characters cannot be satisfied by the usual appeal about heightened universality, for as with Crane's other unconventional methods, there is in his treatment of character an attack on the presumptions about reality found in normal narrative procedures. A man is not defined by his name, but in fiction a name gives an illusion of definition; it suggests existence of an integral personality. Crane threw out methods of characterization which implied that man is constant, integral, and consistent. J. C. Levenson rightly says that Crane "did not sufficiently share nineteenth century premises about character shaping event to affirm or doubt in any complex way that men made history. The principle that moral nature demonstrated itself in conduct meant little to him." [45] The emphasis in Crane's style falls on the constituents of an incident, in which man's instinctive and willed responses, along with chance and circumstance, play partial, unpredictable, and inconclusive roles. In extreme situations, minute distinctions in personality evaporate. Character itself is lost, if we mean by that term a habitual way of harmonizing inner and outer experience; for men suddenly find themselves removed from the realm where habits were formed and where once they might have executed that "unbroken series of successful gestures" [46] that Fitzgerald calls personality. A new context creates a new series of gestures.

Crane's characters are nameless, fragmented, depersonalized, and passive because his attention is usually on that jumble of feeling and sensation that constitutes immediate experience and precedes any sense of self. This is man's normal state; extreme situations only intensify it. Thus momentary states of being and consciousness become more important than action in Crane's character-

izations. A man is defined by what he feels. Emotions become characters and syntactically assume positions in sentences as agents of
action; but emotional states are more complex than language
suggests, and Crane demonstrates this complexity by rendering a
large number of discordant but simultaneous sensations and emotions. Even the simplest gesture may be the product of frothing,
contradictory feelings: "Then the captain, in the bow, chuckled in a
way that expressed humor, contempt, tragedy, all in one" (V, 71).

The effect that feelings have on personality is most extreme when
some intense emotion, particularly rage, forces its way to awareness. How a man sees reveals his state of being. Under intense
emotion, the world falls away, a man loses perspective on his relation to what is around him; but a similar state of depersonalization
also occurs when a man is most aware, when the world is seen in
keenest perspective, when a man becomes most completely and
perfectly himself. At these moments of sensitive attunement, the
characters see with a fullness and clarity that the reader is meant to
share when he, too, apprehends the details as well as the quality of
a scene. All Crane's techniques of style, form, and characterization
can bring a scene or situation to such a still point. Revealed then are
the form and color of an incident. The quality evoked by these revelations—what Coleridge called that "continuous under-current of
feeling . . . everywhere present" [47]—once again defines Crane's
visionary habit of seeing the world as simultaneously ominous and
splendid.

❧ 4 ❧

A SUITABLE SUBJECT:
THE WEST AND THE
WESTERNER

———•••———

*Each boy had, I am sure, a conviction that some day the
wilderness was to give forth to them a marvelous secret.
They felt that the hills and the forest knew much and they
heard a voice of it in the silence. It was vague, thrilling,
fearful and altogether fabulous. The grown folk seemed to
regard these wastes merely as so much distance between
one place and another place or as rabbit cover, or as a
district to be judged according to the value of the timber;
but to the boys it spoke some great inspiriting word which
they knew even as those who pace the shore know the
enigmatic speech of the surf. In the meantime, they lived
there, in season, lives of ringing adventure—by dint
of imagination.* **LYNX-HUNTING**

Whatever personal reasons Crane had for chasing wars (and the
theories advanced have been legion), there remains the haunting
thought that art is not totally cathartic for its maker, that the man of
imagination craves actual testing and fulfillment of his fantastic
projections as a participant in the action. When Crane traveled
through the West and Mexico for Irving Bacheller's syndicate in
1895, he went as a reporter but he brought with him a lifelong fasci-

nation with the land, codes, customs, events, and personages of un-
tamed spaces; his biography is rich with moments of Western role-
playing before and after the trip, and there can be little doubt that
he left the East longing for adventure. His actual participation in
events of the "Wild West" was unexpected and took ironic turns
common to his fiction. His romantic code of honor was put to the
test and routed when he tried to interfere in a barroom fight in Lin-
coln, Nebraska; and he himself, though wearing the regalia of the
Western hero, became the fearful man of his fiction when forced to
flee on horseback from Mexican bandits. The nine tales that came
out of his Western trip include two of the three stories generally
considered to be his best.[1] No doubt direct experience contributed
to the success of his Western stories, but it seems equally true that
in the conventions and even the preposterous clichés of the mythical Wild West Crane found material perfectly suited to the preoc-
cupations of his imagination. In fact, in the story most closely based
on actual experience, "One Dash—Horses," the tale of his adventure with the Mexican bandit Ramon Colorado, Crane goes too far
in his reluctance to take himself 'seriously, and the story's self-
effacement topples into extreme self-consciousness. Experience,
though, is not to be denied. The drama of the real West and Mexico
so aptly coincided with the essential question pervading Crane's
fiction—when can a man trust his own perceptions?— that not only
are these tales among the best of his work, but they offer the truest
account of the fading Wild West to be found in nineteenth-century
American fiction.

Crane's unhesitating embrace of the Western tale as a literary
genre is a further display of his artistic independence and icono-
clasm. Once again he is acting up, following Emerson's advice and
doing something strange in the hallowed corridors of high literature. Not that the West had failed to concern the country's serious
writers. Edwin Fussell has traced its important place in the writings
of Cooper, Hawthorne, Poe, Thoreau, Melville, and Whitman.[2] One
might add Emerson and other writers from Irving to Dana, but
Crane approached his material as though he were the protégé of
Bret Harte rather than the darling of Howells, Conrad, and James.
He wrote of gunfights, attempted lynchings, showdowns, prairie

wars, and cavalry rescues, all the incidents that became staples of the novels of men like Eugene Manlove Rhodes and Zane Grey. The distance of such subjects from literature of high seriousness becomes most pronounced when one realizes that the Western has never acquired even the distinction occasionally conferred on the popular detective story and science fiction.[3] Besides portraying the West as found in those dime novels that reflect the sentiments of Roosevelt, Wister, and Remington, Crane differs from the six authors of Fussell's study in that he visited the places of his fiction.[4] He even differs from those other nineteenth-century writers who did visit the West; unlike Parkman, he was able to put aside his Eastern sensibilities and adopt the Westerner's point of view; and unlike Mark Twain, he avoided the nostalgia and romance that linger beneath that writer's burlesques.

Crane intended to visit the West as early as 1892. In August of that year, after he and his brother were fired from the New York *Tribune*, Crane wrote to the manager of the American Press Association announcing, "I am going south and, also, west this fall and would like to know [sic] I could open up a special article trade with you" (*Letters*, p. 11). The trip was not made until 1895, but the intervening years show that Crane's preconceptions were marked by an intoxication with anticipated glamor and by certain prejudices which he later expressed in an inscription, "To Hamlin Garland of the great honest West, from Stephen Crane of the false East" (*Letters*, p. 126). The West as an idea certainly must have appealed to Crane's admiration for gallant men and gallant animals. In a story written before the trip, "In a Park Row Restaurant," Crane creates a Nevada sheriff who could have marched out of the pages of *Roughing It*. The sheriff speaks of his "life that was full of thrills" and concludes the sketch with a blustering anecdote suitable in its rhythms and audacity to any of Twain's tall tales. Despite the story's parodic details, the Nevada sheriff has size. He dominates the sketch through sheer force of personality, just as the tramp of open spaces in "An Excursion Ticket" is able to catch an audience and "charm them with a description of a journey from Denver to Omaha." Billie Atkins possesses the Western characteristics of persistence and energy, and he can tell "a tale with indescribable gestures and humorous emotions that makes one feel that, after all, the buffets of fate are more comic than otherwise." Unlike those victims of the Bowery whose self-pity is as stiflingly claustrophobic as their environment, Billie Atkins has a wit that matches the judgment made of men by enormous spaces. His actions may come to nothing, and fate may take away everything, but it cannot touch the dignity he maintains through comic self-derision.

Crane's interest in the West grew out of an early reaction to the East. Long before he read Twain or dime novels, or found himself galloping across a desert with a Mexican guide, he had discovered the attractiveness of rural places. As a boy he grew familiar with two distinct social worlds. In his earliest writings, Asbury Park represented a world of comic, phony, and absurd human behavior as opposed to the world of folklore, imagination, and adventure found in less tame Sullivan County. In a sense, Asbury Park and Sullivan County formed the East and West of his early experiential landscape; yet he could approach both without the sentimental prejudice characteristic of much regional literature, for neither place was his true home. His personal preference, though, never left him, and he regularly returned to Sullivan and Pike counties from 1891 to 1895 for summer camping and fishing trips. His early assessment of Asbury Park as a place that "creates nothing. It does not make; it merely amuses" (VIII, 521) was the inchoate response that three years later grew into the general condemnation that "we live for amusement in the east. Damn the east!" (*Letters*, p. 70). Crane's idea of amusement was identified with the "adoration for effete jugs and old kettles" (*Letters*, p. 69), or the seaside antics of the thousands of summer visitors to Asbury Park. Though the West and Sullivan County offered their own forms of amusement, they seemed to attract a different breed; "I have always believed," Crane wrote after his trip, "the western people to be much truer than the eastern people" (*Letters*, p. 69). It is understandable that Crane drew inspiration for his early fiction from the men and animals of Sullivan County. In those stories the hunt is always diminished by Crane's irony, but it still maintains ties to something he found attractive and elemental, a ritualistic confrontation between man and beast, a test of man's skill and nerve—indeed, his manhood—to overcome a worthy adversary. It seems most natural for Crane to have tried to move from Sullivan County to the spacious West in 1892; but forced to wait, he turned to the other geographical pole in his early *Tribune* pieces. Though it was "the unfortunates who have to stay in their crowded tenements" (VIII, 514) that Crane chose as the subject of his first consciously serious writing, he directed the barbs of his fiction toward the bonafide Asbury Parker, who clutched his dollars while comfortably listening to Jacob Riis lecture on "How the Other Half Lives." Little wonder that even after his trip West, Crane qualified his attitudes but still maintained, "I fell in love with the straight out-and-out, sometimes-hideous, often-braggart westerners" (*Letters*, p. 70).

It is perhaps Crane's admiration for "the atmosphere of the west which really is frank and honest" (*Letters*, p. 70) that led him to people it with characters possessing the greatest individuality of any of his fiction's cast of unmemorable characters. Though they still remain stereotypes, his Westerners have faces, costumes, quirks of speech, and histories which invest them with a fictional presence never quite achieved by faceless characters like Maggie. Even the archetypal Marshal Potter, his nameless bride, and that "simple child of the earlier plains," Scratchy Wilson, attain a specificity which by comparison makes Henry Fleming transparent. Crane takes pains to make the hotel keeper Scully talk in the manner he describes: "Scully's speech was always a combination of Irish brogue and idiom, Western twang and idiom, and scraps of curiously formal diction taken from the story-books and newspapers" (V, 154). Making a major exception to his normal practice, Crane devotes an entire section of "A Man and Some Others" to a careful description of sheepherder Bill's life prior to the story. With this emphasis upon characterization also comes a new stress upon the role character plays in relation to event. Life is still basically unknowable and ultimately unmanageable, but personality is given a grander place among the multiple spheres of influence upon action. In "A Poker Game," which is Western in spirit if not in setting, Bobbie Cinch, who is "as generous as sunshine," refuses to raise the ante in a card game because after a string of wins he feels compelled not to take advantage of a "sure thing." He loses, but his generosity saves him from the enormous loss he would have taken if he had been ruled by greed. Though willed actions may not always determine the eventual outcome of an event, they do allow a person some dignity if they are performed as though one were not interested in their result. A person asserts an individual selfhood most fully when operating through a detached and negligible sense of self. In "Moonlight on the Snow," the gambler Larpent chills War Post's natives with a display of disinterested observations about his fate. By treating himself impersonally he achieves an eerie clarity of vision and also paradoxically asserts a unique personal authority that differentiates him from members of the crowd. "He looked handsome and distinguished and—a devil. A devil as cold as moonlight upon the ice."

Despite Crane's bias, parodic details naturally flourish in these tales; "Twelve O'Clock" and "Moonlight on the Snow" might be read as parodies of Bret Harte. Crane was too realistic to accept the dime novel portrayal of the Western hero as always fair and square, generous, competent, fearless, and triumphant. "Garland," he wrote, "will wring every westerner by the hand and hail him as a frank honest man. I wont. No, sir" (Letters, p. 70). It is difficult, though, to accept parody as the main intention of the stories. Too many figures of the mythical West are ignored. Though they present themselves as easy targets, Crane makes no attempt to deflate wagon masters, road agents, scouts, hunters, trappers, miners, Texas rangers, Indian heroines, counterfeiters, or those popular subjects of the 1890s dime novel, which, Henry Nash Smith says, "had come to hinge almost entirely upon conflict between detectives and bands of robbers." [5] Crane wrote mostly about characters he might have met on his trip, or who still might have lingered around the West of the 1890s, even as anachronisms. He introduces the city kids in "The Wise Men" and "The Five White Mice," not so much as embodiments of the East-West conflict that was such a popular theme with Twain, but as humorous exemplars of the effect adaptations to Western style might have on character and action. In writing realistically about the West, Crane naturally criticizes the myths spawned by potboilers, but not as a primary intention. "One Dash—Horses" might indirectly ridicule the "usual Western hero

[who] is not afraid," [6] but its main purpose is to render the psychological and emotional truth of a moment in which the protagonist freezes into a pose of Western calm, leaving his antagonists uncertain whether "he was a great fighter; or perhaps . . . an idiot." The apparent "envelope of ridicule of Western myth" [7] enclosing these events is really, as suggested earlier, the self-conscious ridicule Crane directed toward himself and his real-life flight from bandits. The comic gestures of this story are less parodic than they are expressions of the Western attitude shared by Billie Atkins in the self-derisive and scornful stance he takes toward his own misadventures. Despite its popularity as a subject for critical exegeses, the discrepancy between the real West and its myth, which generates the plot of "The Blue Hotel," is the most obvious and least interesting of Crane's Western observations. As in the best of his other fiction, Crane was more interested in the disturbing implications generated by the "conflict of the two perceptions" (VIII, 324). Even in "The Last of the Mohicans," written when he was nineteen, he juxtaposes against Cooper's romantic creation the claim that "the real and only authentic last of the Mohicans, was a demoralized, dilapidated inhabitant of Sullivan County" (VIII, 199). At this point Crane does not rest with an easily accomplished parody. He does not let "truth" overwhelm "fiction," or fiction cancel fiction, but moves beyond questions of historical truth to dwell on "the pathos [that] lies in the contrast between the noble savage of fiction and the sworn-to claimant of Sullivan County." This same pathos underlies his comic characterization of Scratchy Wilson acting as though he were still part of the old gang that used to hang out along the river.

Crane's incorporation of stock figures and stock situations into his Western tales actualized the implicit conceptions of his art. A prose determined by a conviction that experience is incoherent and unpredictable could find no more suitable subjects than those of Westerns, which, as Eric Solomon says, even among the "more serious writers also leaned heavily on melodramatic devices and devious plot twists." [8] The unexpected rescue by Mexican *rurales* in "One Dash—Horses" is a cliché of Western literature and film, but this event of pure chance actually happened. It is an example not only of life imitating artistic conventions, but of life justifying the lack of causal relationships in Crane's hesitant and fragmented style. When Crane's occasional wrenchings of words and syntax produce shocks exceeding their meanings, the effect is no more gratuitous or melodramatic than when Big Watson in "Twelve O'Clock" shoots an innocent hotelkeeper through the throat. Unlike *Maggie,* where violence is forced, and unlike the war fiction where violence is given, the Western stories come closest to the essential subject defined by his style. In all Westerns (and in Crane's conception of experience), there is usually "an element of violence"; but as Bernard DeVoto remarks, "it may be not overt but latent or perhaps only conceptual." [9] The settings of Western fiction—the vast, impersonal spaces, the enormous sky, the scrubby ranges subject to drought and storm—were all the scenery Crane needed for realistic staging of his conception of man's spiritual plight. There are no majestic mountains, rushing white waters, or prairies glistening with waist-high buffalo grass in the Western stories, only the flat and desolate landscape and sluggish rivers of the West Crane actually visited. In "One Dash—Horses," Crane even adopts the familiar trope, going back to Irving and Cooper, of comparing the plain to a sea, but in his fiction that expanse becomes charged with all the meaning found in the sea of "The Open Boat." In "A Man and Some Others," the limitless stretch of mesquite is the stage on which the protagonists of many of Crane's poems find themselves: "the world was declared to be a desert and unpeopled." The storm in "The Blue Hotel" makes the same declaration, but the Swede reacts to it as do many writers and readers of standard Western fiction: " 'Yes, I like this weather. I like it. It suits me.' It was apparently his design to impart a deep significance to these words." Such storms are conventions in Western myth, and like the mountains and plains, they naturally diminish man but also test him. The Swede's "deep significance" was that he was a man to match those mountains and storms. Crane uses the convention, but its function is larger than the usual one; the storm is like the prairie; the men from the hotel "plunged into the tempest as into a sea," and the Swede "tacked across the face of the storm as if he carried sails." The storm emphasizes man's situation and offers disparaging comment on his efforts, but it is also a real storm that acts as a catalyst for psychological revelations. Typical of Crane's method, the storm is also a transformative agent that alters the historical and social reality of Fort Romper and lifts it to a new dimension; the Swede then "might have been in a deserted village. . . . here, with the bugles of the tempest pealing, it was hard to imagine a peopled earth."

Anyone who has been subjected to the primitive enormousness of the West, or has even read hymns to its expanse knows that its effect on the individual is both disquieting and enhancing. Unlike many other writers, Crane could not comfortably praise the West's grandeur. For in human terms, the plains, mountains, and canyons brutally diminish man and force him to accept a nontragic view of existence which the self-aggrandizing social complexities of the East blindly negate. Among these spaces a man knows that he is not really at home in his world and must live in continual acknowledgement of his own lack of consequence, a view that pervades Crane's Western stories and finds its embodiment in Bill's indifferent reaction to Miguel, whom he has just killed. Unable to be completely serious, a person can only mock events or affect disinterest, as do the gambler Larpent and the narrator of these tales. The stock situations of Western myth are causes of further reduction. A senseless blast from Big Watson's revolver or a stray bullet from Scratchy Wilson's or, as in earlier literature, the flash of an Indian's scalping knife merely objectify what inhabitants of the West already know about their condition. The weather, too, as Crane reported in "Nebraska's Bitter Fight for Life," comes in extremes: the winds may be "wolves of ice" or "hot as an oven's fury," leaving the prairie "bleak and desolate" and the people "helpless." Real conditions in the West depersonalize man, and so do the violent conventions of Western fiction; both reality and literary genre, then, gave support to Crane's earlier ways of presenting characters as fragments, machines, and animals. Yet the West is nothing if not contradictory. It enhances man. Landscape and events do not rob a person of his sense of self as rapidly as do crowds in a congested city; they actually heighten that sense. In a report from Mexico, Crane mocks the hats, shirts, and spurs that exceed their functional use, but these items also act as assertions of individuality and vitality in face of the impersonal. All the trappings of the cowboy and vaquero and buckaroo serve the same purpose, as do Crane's studied character-izations of Scully, Larpent, Bill, Scratchy, Pop, Big Watson, Richardson, and José. To the townsmen of Fort Romper, Scully "performed a feat" when he painted his hotel a splendid blue "that made the dazzling winter landscape of Nebraska seem only a gray swampish hush." While the assertive gear, actions, and poses of Westerners may be only further reflections of the "conceit of man," Crane knew that this conceit was also "the very engine of life" (V, 165).

The Western loner became the perfect protagonist for a fiction whose vocabulary and rhetoric were most adept at describing an in-dividual's responses to his world. Concentrated moments, the prime subject of all Crane's best fiction, are the rule of life for char-acters such as Bill, a former cowboy who, like most cowboys of Western myth, thrived on sensation for its own sake. Unlike other stereotypes of the West, the cowboy and various offshoots of that nomadic culture did not find themselves chronicled until the end of the nineteenth century and the beginning of the next, when the works of Andy Adams, Owen Wister, and Alfred Henry Lewis began to appear between hard covers. But for Crane, the cowboy or the desperado—or even a dude like Richardson, who affects the style and outfit of the cowboy—became a true exemplum of isola-ted, unaccommodated man, a truer protagonist for Crane's fiction than even the soldier, for despite Fleming's feelings of isolation, he is always a member of a regiment, a social group. The sheepherder, Bill, belongs to nothing even remotely resembling a regiment. Sepa-rated from conventional society, the wanderer perceives the world around him and judges it according to the stark frame of reference that always attracted Crane. This state of mind, devoid of the nor-mal assumptions of social man, displays its peculiarity and primi-tiveness in something as basic as the conception of time. In the desert of "A Man and Some Others," "There was no owl-faced clock to chant the weariness of the long silence that brooded upon the plain." The shift in perspective and the subsequent alteration of re-ality that social conventions effect on Marshal Potter is expressed less in his manners toward his new bride than in his consciousness of civilization's imposing measurement and judgment. "We are due in Yellow Sky at 3.42," he tells his wife, and talks of "the little silver watch" he bought for her. Unwittingly responding in like manner to the new eyes Potter has acquired, his bride announces, "It's seventeen minutes past twelve."

The landscape of the West and its weather, a poignant reminder that life takes place on a "whirling, fire-smote, ice-locked, disease-stricken, space-lost bulb" (V, 165), also starkly exposes the dynamics of man's communal forms. The mere existence of a blue hotel and a saloon on a vast plain and in an overwhelming storm forces a reader's reassessment of the nature of society. Without having to fight through tradition-bound conceptions, Crane can dramatize the arbitrariness and fragility of social configurations that might automatically be taken for granted in the context of the city or the city novel. Time, as well as setting, works dramatically, for while the darker forces of city life had long become encrusted with rationalizations of morality and refinement, the bare framework of society in the West was being viewed at its inception. Even in the 1890s civilization in the West was still thin enough to show that it grew from roots of vice as much as virtue. In "Moonlight on the Snow," when the angel of peace vies with the devils of violence and greed, there is real question as to who is the seducer and who is the seduced.

In moving toward the elemental, Crane stripped inessentials from experience and burrowed into its core. There he found Henry Fleming and Timothy Lean staring into the blank eyes of corpses. In the West he found that a man was not always compelled to choose a confrontation either with the eyes of dead individuals or with the many eyes of a monster army, but like the Kid in "The Five White Mice," he could look into the eyes of a living being and see there the darker churnings of his own soul.

The mythic showdown of the Wild West provided Crane with the intense moments that were his favorite subject, and the circumstances of their occurrence released the basic primitive emotions and archetypal realizations that social conventions kept in the closet. According to Crane's private mythology, man's fundamental antagonist is the snake; it arouses fear, repulsion, and rage in their purest and most elemental form.

> In the formation of devices hideous and horrible, nature reached her supreme point in the making of the snake, so that priests who really paint hell well fill it with snakes instead of fire. [VIII, 66–67]

The flaming chemicals that permanently transform Henry Johnson into The Monster coalesce into "a ruby-red snakelike thing" before they swim and "with mystic impulse" flow onto his upturned face. In the Western stories snakes and reptiles frequently appear in connection with revelations of man's elemental self and his fundamental conflicts. Richardson, in "One Dash—Horses," is frightened to immobility by a "fat, round-faced Mexican, whose little snake-like mustache was as black as his eyes." Later, when the man reoccupies Richardson's memory, the detail of the "mustache like a snake" is recalled. Sheepherder Bill's enemies move like "monster lizards" toward his camp, "gliding with the finesse of the escaping serpent." To Bill his revolver is "the poison of the snake"; when he aims at his enemies it is "poised like the glittering crest of a snake." Normally harmless Scratchy Wilson becomes transformed when drunk; he thrusts "his revolver venomously forward"; and the young bride in Yellow Sky becomes "a slave to hideous rites, gazing at the apparitional snake." When the New York Kid pulls his pistol on his antagonist, "the cry of the grandee was that of a man who suddenly sees a poisonous snake."

Western situations also gave Crane a natural setting in which to examine human fear, especially the fear of death. Throughout his fiction there is a basic pattern which begins in the Sullivan County Tales with the little man's conviction, "He knew he was going to be eaten" (VIII, 266). Dan Emmonds shares the little man's fears, and after his rescue from a shipwreck, addresses himself, "Devil knows what kind of a stew you will make for these grinning barbarians." [10] In *The Red Badge,* the cause for such trepidation is more pronounced, but the terminology remains the same. Facing a Confederate charge, a soldier voices the fears of his comrades, "We'll git swallowed" (*RB,* 276).[11] None of these characters are swallowed, but in the Western tales, as Crane moves closer to confronting what these men fear, the threats become more realistic, and the characters' projections are no longer masked behind imagery of being eaten. The Kid in "The Five White Mice," "suddenly decided he was going to be killed." In "The Blue Hotel," the shaky Swede confronts the card players: " 'Gentlemen,' he quavered, 'I suppose I am going to be killed before I can leave this house.' " The Swede's pronouncement is inaccurate only in its specifics; in a ramshackle town of the West, Crane finally pursues the little man's projections to their ultimate realization.

In the earlier tales such moments of fear become ridiculous and enshrouded in comedy, but the humor is uneasy and rarely provokes laughter. All the Western tales are comic or streaked with comedy, but this habit does not nullify the seriousness of the moments examined. When Richardson feels his "knee joints turn to bread," there is little reason to suspect Crane is parodying the fearless Western hero.[12] In his report about the New Orleans opera, he uncharacteristically reveals a few qualities he seems to demand from any art, and one is "emotional sincerity" (VIII, 427). A definition of emotion negatively achieved through mocking reference to romance is still a mode of asserting a positive description through contrast, as in this passage from "A Man and Some Others":

> A romance relates the tale of the black cell hidden deep in the earth, where, upon entering, one sees only the little eyes of snakes fixing him in menaces. If a man could have approached a certain spot in the bushes, he would not have found it romantically necessary to have his hair rise. There would have been sufficient expression of horror in the feeling of the death-hand at the nape of his neck and in his rubber knee joints. [V, 61]

Observed with common sense, this moment would be no more than a scene of advancing enemies and possible death; but it is recalled that Crane identifies snakes with hell, the moment is another example of his propensity to choose situations which illuminate life as essentially hellish. These are the powers that exist normally unseen even in Maggie's world. The sheepherder then intensifies the experience when he lets out "a fearsome laugh of ridicule, hatred, feroc-

ity. It might have been demoniac." Crane was not so naïve as to
think that fear was unfounded in such situations. To see his fearful
men only as parodic characters is to dimish his psychological penetration. Even the "bravest" of men know fear, but it doesn't stop
them from pursuing danger. And to say that Crane was "mainly
inclined to define and dramatize fear as anything the coward per-
mitted to interfere with courage" [13] is another oversimplification.
No one would say that the Kid from New York in "The Five White
Mice" is a coward, but his ability to stand up to his potential assassin stems no more from his sense of "honorable manhood" than
from his fear—an "inability prevented him from running away."

In the Western stories Crane probes deeper than he had before
into conceptions of honor, bravery, fear, and the personality of the
stoic veteran. From the inception of his career, he knew that all
fears, whether of dark caves, heights, speed, bullets, were really
fears of the unknown. "It is mightier than the war yell of the dreadful, because the dreadful may be definite" (VIII, 256). Rage supplants fear when its cause is trivial and expectations are unfulfilled.
Released from immediate threat, Richardson reflects that "there was
a certain fat Mexican . . . who came extremely near to have eaten
his last tamale merely because he frightened a man too much."
Just as the matador El Cordobés, after being gored by the first bull
he had faced in Madrid, claimed, "It wasn't the pain I was worried
about, it was the fear," [14] Crane's characters often hate their fear
more than actual threats. The blanket over the door fascinates
Richardson, becomes "a horrible emblem, and a horrible thing in
itself" because it hides the ultimate unknown, "the black and silver
coffins, all the panoply of death." Using the most fundamental
terms to dramatize man's possible responses to the fearsome, Crane
shows in "The Snake" that a man is moved not by courage but by
his natural impulse to go "sheer raving mad from the emotions of
his fore-fathers." The dude in "A Man and Some Others" is transformed during a gunfight, and "a panther is at the time born in the
heart." He discovers "that it was easy to kill a man," but this
thought "went swiftly by him." After the gun battle, when he becomes a "man" again, he recognizes the horror of what has oc-

curred; "all at once he made a gesture of fright and looked wildly about him."

In "The Five White Mice," Crane begins to explore causes of provocation and subsequent rage peculiar to the individual. One of the Kid's opponents has his back bent "in the supposed manner of a Spanish grandee. This concave gentleman cut a fine and terrible figure. The lad, moved by the spirits of his modest and perpendicular ancestors, had time to feel his blood roar at sight of the pose." In other stories Crane looks more closely at why men respond differently to the same situation, but in "Mice" he introduces humorously the idea that what men may claim as individual character is shaped as much by inherited prejudices, moralities, and customs as it is by physical heredity or environmental conditioning. Still, it is the degree to which a situation is unknown that most influences individual responses. The bride becomes a slave to hideous rites and gazes at an apparitional snake in Yellow Sky only because she does not realize how much of a game is the ritual encounter between her husband and Wilson. If it were not, one or the other would have been dead long before this moment when Potter changes the rules by appearing armed only with a wife. Wilson needs Potter, the only man who will participate in his fantasies, and Potter, apparently capable of ending this rite if he willed, has chosen instead to shoot "Wilson up once—in the leg."

The Western stories also clarify to what a large extent "courage" consists of nothing more than realistic knowledge and technique. Bill, a veteran of many battles—unlike his visitor, who is a mere recruit—knows that their enemies have not scampered, as the Easterner has claimed. This knowledge keeps them alive. Of all the virtues honored by members of a cowboy culture, the most immediately sought is competence; and all such virtues are honored tacitly: "It was their absence," Wallace Stegner says, "not their presence, that was cause for remark." [15] Bill relaxes as soon as he perceives that his new visitor is a greenhorn who rides with his arches hooked in the stirrups. Confidence is not blind; Bill, like Scratchy Wilson, is a whiz with a revolver, but before venturing into a dangerous situation, he drew his revolver from its old holster "and examined every part of it." Knowing that there will be an attempt to murder him during the night, he molds his blanket over utensils and other items to form a dummy body, and waits for the attack on the outskirts of the camp. Knowledge of exactly what he has to fear reduces that fear, and extensive precautions before confronting the cause of it diminish the actual danger—just as in *The Red Badge* it is the veterans, not the recruits, who dig in "like terriers" (*RB*, 218–19) even when danger is not apparent. These are the qualities that separate the "fearless" man from youth locked in ignorance and terror of the unknown. Richardson displays his incompetence when he straps on noisy spurs before sneaking away from bandits; and though Big Watson's murder of the hotelkeeper is senseless and immoral, according to the code of the West the hotel owner brought death upon himself by presuming to hold two revolvers in "incompetent hands." The veteran appraises the reality of his danger, follows certain rules, and attains as much control of a situation as his competence allows; beyond that, he is no different from other men in whose hearts a panther may be born. Confronted with an experience about which he knows nothing, a novice may resort to magical incantations, as does the Kid with his ditty about the five white mice. Like Henry Fleming's fairytale delusions, or the impulse to talk to oneself, these tics may produce an illusion of control (and even sufficiently rectify a psychological disorder to allow a man to function), but they have no real effect on the reality outside the individual. The gamblers in "The Five White Mice" grow impatient with one man's "rites" as he applies "the magic of deliberation" and blows softly into the dice cup. A veteran of the plains, knowing what he can and cannot control, takes his turn with the dice quite differently: "An American, tall and with a face of copper red from the rays that flash among the Sierra Madres and burn on the cactus deserts, took the little leathern cup and spun the dice out upon the polished wood."

It is not necessarily a death wish that compels certain men to take unaccountable risks. By developing skills to minimize danger, veterans make it a habit of doing everything in their power to stay alive. Also, when a man voluntarily enters a situation of unnecessary exposure to death—an act that can be seen as simultaneously

courageous and foolish—he does not always have the highest mo-
tives. Simple pride, Crane knows, can sting a man into a desire to
distinguish himself from mass man; like Henry Fleming, few men
want to be shuffled off as part of a blue demonstration. There is
always a certain perverse pleasure in accepting a challenge no matter how nonsensical it may be. The little man of Sullivan County,
uncontrollably responsive to the shouts of his vanity, continually
finds himself in ridiculous situations, just as Collins, in "A Mystery
of Heroism," accepts the taunts of his comrades and discovers that
he does not know whether he is a hero or a fool. Jibes, insults, any
diminishing of personal stature can so fill up one's consciousness
that there is no room for selflessness. Fleming fights like a wildcat,
enraged at an overheard judgment of himself as a mule driver and
in his fury wishing only vengeance on the man who uttered it. The
veteran Bill, angered by his enemies' evaluation of himself as "a
dog that sneaked," as well as other base beings, has to be warned
by a greenhorn not to "budge an inch" and to put his head down.
Crane shows how often "courageous" acts stem from lavish fights
of vanity, and how often pure prideful anger can overwhelm other
emotions, including fear.

Moments of extreme tension, encounters where the only prize is
life, are not altogether unsalutary. Daredevils, adventurers, and
soldiers know the pleasure of competence exercised as even a minimal assertion of control in situations where forces normally make
men their pawns. And as we have seen, fear itself, like anger, can
be exhilerating. When the New York Kid feels his first close touch
with death, he experiences a sensuous appreciation of the sheer fact
of living that is unavailable in moments when death is only an abstraction. The moment of fear may be the moment when man's
senses are most alive, as Richardson knows when he orders his
guide to follow him at fifty paces:

> Richardson had resolved in his rage that at any rate he was going to
> use the eyes and ears of extreme fear to detect the approach of
> danger; and so he established his servant as a sort of an outpost. [V,
> 22]

These same quick eyes and ears, the invigorated perceptors, seem
responsible for the transformative moments when Crane's scenes

appear like apparitions in the night. Of all the Western stories, up to and including "The Blue Hotel," only the climactic scene of "The Bride Comes to Yellow Sky" takes place in daylight; all the other important scenes are staged either at night or as if at night. The second gun battle of "A Man and Some Others" occurs in the morning, but the quick presentation of action, the "rush of feet, the spatter of shots, the cries, the swollen faces seen like masks on the smoke, resembled a happening of the night." Similarly, in the two Western tales written after "The Blue Hotel," the events are described with nighttime imagery. The shooting in "Twelve O'Clock" occurs at noon but it elicits a shriek "like windy, midnight death"; and in the middle of the day, Larpent shines with distinction, like "Moonlight on the Snow." Crane praised the "dramatic comprehension" he found in a soprano's singing in the New Orleans opera; his own dramatic comprehension in the Western stories included not only the drama of event but also the drama of color and form; his unearthly visualizations of action, as much as the action itself, gave his Westerns the "dash and vigor," "snap and intensity" he found so admirable in the New Orleans opera chorus (VIII, 427). Appearing as night apparitions, his scenes define experience as fleeting and elusive; they avoid the "candor of breaking day" that makes events uninteresting. Instead these manipulations of color and form are meant to "slit with a dagger's sweep the curtain of commonplace" (VIII, 383).

These energetic dramatizations also embody the psychological realities of the unearthly moments they project. Western situations were favorable toward Crane's propensity to stop time and to explore the energies of a moment. A new complexity entered his fiction, evident in the extended probings during Richardson's and the Kid's moments of fright. The innovations of his short fiction effected a radical change in the uses Crane made of stock Western situations. Exterior events, such as a murder, are seen to yield less information about the true nature of experience than do interior and normally invisible ones. The shift in fictional conception is profound. What is important in experience is no longer great, discernible turning points; the hanging of Larpent in "Moonlight on the Snow" is treated as "a detail in a set of circumstances." Even the trivial or the nonevent can offer an active definition of man's dimensions and his relationship to other people, geography, and life in general if that nonevent is seriously explored—as in "The Five White Mice," where the nonviolent resolution of a potentially explosive situation is the culmination of a dazzling string of trivial and ironic occurrences, any of which, if altered, might have shaped a quite different public event. If the Kid had won at dice, he might have gotten drunk with his friends and lost the confrontation in the alley. In a way a loss has become a victory. Crane has become even more interested in the "why's" and "if's" behind observable phenomena, and he is more careful in delineating them.

The Western scenes and actions and the formal patterns they evolve seem ready-made for a style that is abrupt, elliptical, nervous, and swift. But with the appearance of the Western story, "One Dash—Horses," there came a major change in Crane's prose which eventually led to what Berryman called "the supple majesty" of "The Open Boat." Absent are the extreme verbal excesses and syntactic dislocations of *The Red Badge*. A new fluidity and a new impassiveness, a firm narrative control, and an imaginative restraint temper these tales of chance and violence. It is as if Crane had adopted the laconic habits of Western speech. One can imagine Crane's delight even amid the pain he felt for the storm-ravaged inhabitants of Nebraska when he asked the stricken farmer how he got along without aid or money. "Don't git along, stranger" (VIII, 418), was the man's reply, a response slick enough in its gap between speech and feeling to have been invented by Crane himself; it is an example of the understated style he exploits in his later fiction. It is a style which embodies the self-reliance, discipline, perspective, pride, stoicism, and sense of individuality Crane thought were the attributes of Westerners, a sum of attitudes compressed into the code evoked in Owen Wister's famous sentence, "When you call me that, smile!" [16] Western speech specifically marked by bluffs, indirection, understatement, and teasing eschews self-pity, but it is also a protective strategy, a challenge to others to expose their vulnerability without jeopardizing one's own fragile control of self and situation. As a style it honors emotional privacy and self-assurance, masks weaknesses, and acknowledges the basic ineffectuality of words in situations of any moment. " 'This comes from discussin' things,' cried Bill angrily" when his attackers catch him off guard (V, 64).

The tight-lipped utterances of Western actors in myth and reality as well as the bold, wooden-faced exaggerations and bluffs give voice to a code whose purest style is found at the card table and whose master is the professional gambler. Every time they ply their trade, Larpent in "Moonlight on the Snow" and the gambler in "The Blue Hotel" subject themselves to the vicissitudes of chance, but they are veterans; they know the odds and, confident of their skills, they control themselves, even though the situations in which they are involved escape ultimate control. As a natural part of Western life, gambling and the gambler's code dramatize a concept of experience metaphorically present throughout Crane's fiction. Besides foolish curiosity, the impetus for the entanglements of the Sullivan County tales is often the bet or dare, a mode of frontier bravado. A poker game climaxes "Four Men in a Cave," while "A Ghoul's Accountant" ends with a pseudoriddle to which the little man gives the correct answer, but to no avail; he is kicked anyway. The little man is constantly swindled, literally and emotionally, just as Uncle Jake is swindled by the town dealer, King Cetewayo by his visitors, and the natives by colonizers in "A Foreign Policy, in Three Glimpses." The game and the swindle became staple motifs in Crane's fiction and exemplified his larger theme of life swindling man's expectations of it. All this comes into the open in the Western tales, and those few stories that do not treat gambling directly are still often presented in gambling terms. The title "One Dash— Horses" conceives of Richardson's dash for life as an all-or-nothing "dash," which is Western slang for a single roll of dice.[17]

The gambling culture of the West is not unrelated to various activities of daring and chance that found their embodiments in out-of-door adventures and college sports of the 1890s. Crane's description of a poker game, with a few changes, might serve to define that moment when the little man takes aim at a bear, or even when the sportsman Crane awaited a hot clothesliner on the baseball diamond; "here a year's reflection is compressed into a moment of thought, here the nerves may stand on end and scream to themselves, but a tranquility as from heaven is only interrupted by the click of chips. The higher the stakes the more quiet the scene; this is a law that applies everywhere save on the stage" (V, 192). Crane's attraction to moments that test men's nerve and skill, to hunting and camping, baseball and football, puts him in league with a Theodore Roosevelt, who could pronounce "that our country calls not for the life of ease, but for the life of strenuous endeavor." Roosevelt's rationale for the strenuous life was that "if we shrink from the hard contests where men must win at hazard of their lives and at the risk of all they hold dear, then the bolder and stronger peoples will pass us by and will win for themselves the domination of the world." [18] But Crane was too intelligent to accept this as fact. Roosevelt's social Darwinism is closer to the views of Yale's William Graham Sumner and of Walter Camp, the father of American football, finding its ultimate reduction in contemporary sports where, according to a Vince Lombardi, "winning is the only thing." [19] To Crane it did not matter so much that the Kids in "The Wise Men" happened to win and that Bill in "A Man and Some Others" lost; his attitude was closely allied to a more honorable assessment of the manner of competition, and to the mixture of emotion and thought during the competition. Though Crane could find parallels between sport and experience in general, he realized that as a codification of life, sports could not completely encompass the brutal messiness and evasions of daily experience. According to F. Scott Fitzgerald it was just such a search for a sporting paradigm of experience that left Ring Lardner an uneducated man:

> It was never that [Lardner] was completely sold on athletic virtuosity as the be-all and end-all of problems; the trouble was that he could find nothing finer. Imagine life conceived as a business of beautiful muscular organization—an arising, an effort, a good break, a sweat, a bath, a meal, a love, a sleep—imagine it achieved; then imagine trying to apply that standard to the horribly complicated mess of living, where nothing, even the greatest conceptions and workings and achievements, is else but messy, spotty, tortuous— and then one can imagine the confusion that Ring faced on coming out of the ball park.[20]

Crane's knowledge that the fittest did not always survive, and that accommodation to and even mastery of rules did not guarantee success to the boldest, led him to write Westerns where horse-opera heroes experienced fear and even lost gunfights. Roosevelt's ideas about the strenuous life were quite different; in a letter to Crane he objected to Bill's death in "A Man and Some Others" and advised Crane, "Some day I want you to write another story of the frontiersman and the Mexican Greaser in which the frontiersman shall come out on top; it is more normal that way!" (*Letters*, p. 128).

Readers in the 1890s wanted the West to remain romantic. So did Crane, but his honesty to his perceptions would not let him simplify the roles and actions of Westerners as did Buffalo Bill's Wild West Show, nor would he create Owen Wister's kind of hero, "a sun god in leather pants." As Bernard DeVoto said, "The actual prototype of the gun for hire was a repulsive psychopath like anyone who carried a submachine gun for Al Capone"; [21] and that is exactly how Crane presents Big Watson in "Twelve O'Clock." Sheepherder Bill, a former mine owner and cowboy, is also a murderer; and as a bouncer in the Bowery and a brakeman on the Union Pacific, "he practised all the ordinary cruelties upon these other creatures of ill fortune." [22] The cowboy and his culture have been so romanticized since the nineteenth century that we must be reminded of how he was viewed in his own time:

> As late as 1881 . . . the pejorative connotations of the term "cowboy" were still uppermost. President Chester A. Arthur's first Annual Message to Congress mentioned a disturbance of the public tranquility by a band of "armed desperadoes known as 'Cowboys' probably numbering from fifty to one hundred men," who had for months been committing acts of lawlessness and brutality in the Territory of Arizona, and across the border in Mexico. He asked for legislation empowering the Army to intervene. [23]

The West Crane visited was a tamer place than readers of dime novels would suspect, and yet he included in his tales many of the mythical aspects of the West and stereotyped characters such as Scratchy Wilson and the cowboy in "The Blue Hotel" not only because Eastern readers expected them, but because they were actual presences in the West of the 1890s, a West that was as much a creation of its inhabitants' exaggeration and posturing as it was of Eastern gullibility. As any present-day visitor to the West or a rodeo knows, "Westerners" are only too happy to act out the scenarios of their own and their visitors' fantasy. Even today, many Westerners and cowboys live by a code anachronistically unresponsive to the actual conditions of their lives. Crane's experience in Sullivan County had made him wary of the Wild West of the imagination that officially began on July 4, 1882, when Cody was appointed the first grand marshal of an "old Glory Blowout" in North Platte, Nebraska. When he was only twenty, Crane showed he knew that for a "city man" Western ways were not much different from "The Ways in Sullivan County."

> After he recovers from a paroxysm of awe and astonishment he seizes his pen and with flashing eye and trembling, eager fingers, writes those brief but lurid sketches which fascinate and charm the reading public while the virtuous bushwacker, whittling a stick near by smiles in his own calm and sweet fashion. [VIII, 220–21]

Despite his own posturing as a Westerner, Crane knew exactly what he was and exactly what kind of West he visited. Even on the barren plains of southwestern Texas in 1895, he said, "one is in danger of meeting horse-thieves or tourists" (V, 58).

Crane's tales attain a social and historical accuracy because he held no allegiance to a Rooseveltian need to romanticize the West, nor did he feel compelled, as did Richard Harding Davis, merely to spoof "the mild west." [24] His ironic disinterest allowed him to chart the contradictions in a person like Bill, who could simultaneously exhibit the West's legendary hospitality and the American trait of suspicion and brutality toward everyone. Crane could dissect what was honorable from a code of life that was basically limited and inhumane. He established no easy dichotomy between the natural man of the West and the social man of the East. Even in the West he found an adaptation of custom and ceremony that his comic sense let him regard with the same disinterest he showed toward the ways of the millionaire in "An Experiment in Luxury." Accepting the Wild West as a passing thing, he refuses to be retrospectively nostalgic over what might have been lost and does not hesitate to present the retired but still competent desperado, Scratchy Wilson, as ludicrous. Yet "The Bride Comes to Yellow Sky" is more than a parable of civilization's encroachment upon the

West.[25] It encompasses a larger theme found generally in Crane's fiction, a theme for which ceremony and chaos might serve as descriptive polarities.

The ceremony of teacups in "The Monster" is the normal ritual that veils the citizens of Whilomville from the starker biological and metaphysical realities of their lives. Though participation in such a ceremony may be only the guise of decency, it is still a stay against chaos or against the nothingness Fleming faces when he fails to abide by the rituals of regimental combat. Ceremony may be reduced to a game; the barkeeper of The Weary Gentleman saloon instructs the visiting drummer in the rules to be followed when Scratchy "gets on one of these tears." Everyone is safe because the drunken gunfighter "can't break down that door." When Potter violates the rules of their ritualistic gunfight by appearing unarmed, Scratchy's "face went livid." Momentarily unaware that a new set of customs will prevent the chaos he expects, Potter abides by the old rules and awaits his death; his "heels had not moved an inch backward." But with the announcement of marriage, the game is up, and Wilson, bound to a womanless, nomadic, basically romantic culture, "went away." The "funnel-shaped" tracks he leaves in the sand have been seen as symbolic hourglasses, since time has run out for Scratchy,[26] but they are first a visually accurate description of boot tracks. The implication of their ephemerality is no less applicable to the boots that Potter himself wears, for the marshal's uncomfortable adaptation of another culture's customs and ceremonies is mocked in the first part of the story with same gentleness as are the rituals of Yellow Sky. As later in "Moonlight on the Snow" and "The Blue Hotel," one mode of creating order in the face of chaos has replaced another; though both have been necessary, neither is inclusive or powerful enough to enable man to understand or control his essential condition. Violence, injustice, and chaos can break through the ways of civilization as easily as they do through the ways of barbarism. Who is to say which ceremonial forms are more honest and better suited to the realities of existence, and to the individual's need to function in a world where struggle and death are often the only certainties?

In "The Blue Hotel," Crane anatomizes the social structure of the

Western town, and in the process he transcends local conditions and clarifies the complex relationships of fantasy, will, circumstance, environment, chance, and social rule he had begun to explore in *Maggie*. In this, the best of his Western stories, he manages to balance all the forces impinging on event so that no single causal development can explain away the Swede's murder without ignoring or seriously distorting other reasons for the death.[27] "The Blue Hotel" forces more double takes upon the reader than any other Crane story; and while it may be said that the mystery of the story is the mystery of experience, there simultaneously occurs the illumination offered only by literature of the highest rank, for the reader is made aware of the distinct elements comprising what is ultimately an impenetrable experience. Fort Romper is further along in its social transitions than was Yellow Sky; the hotelkeeper Scully insists that "in two years Romper'll be a met-tro-*pol*-is." He cites the imminent appearance of electric streetcars, four churches, a new railroad, a school house, and a factory—all the institutions that had brought the frontier to an official close by 1890 and which, by implication, would bring with them the law and civility of the East, forever altering the West in everything except, as the story shows, the violence of nature and of man. Crane's presentation of these homogenizing processes, which began with Scratchy Wilson's apparel (the cowboy shirt made in New York and the boots like those worn by boys in New England), gives his portrait of the West an authenticity lacking in stories by other writers who were attracted only to what was distinctively colorful and eccentric about the West. Few readers and writers wanted to admit with Crane that "travellers tumbling over each other in their haste to trumpet the radical differences between Eastern and Western life have created a generally wrong opinion. . . . It is this fact which has kept the sweeping march of the West from being chronicled in any particularly true manner" (VIII, 474–75). For this reason, in his report about Galveston, Crane emphasizes that it is "not like a town in the moon. There are, of course, a thousand details of street color and life which are thoroughly typical of any American city" (VIII, 475). Fort Romper is not yet a Galveston, but it has what appears in "Moonlight on the Snow" and "Twelve O'Clock" as the first and

most important institution of civilization—a hotel. The Swede is
not alone in his inclination to deny the progressive taming of the
West that has at least partially occurred; Scully's son, Johnnie, is
just as caught up in visions of the Wild West, only he places his
projections of *"Out West"* in Wyoming, and it takes the traveled
Easterner to correct him; "It isn't different there even—not in these
days." The Wild West is a relative thing; the Easterner identifies it
as "right in the middle of hell," which Crane knows can be found
in New York or Whilomville as well as in Fort Romper, Nebraska.

As in *Maggie,* where Crane first emphasized the psychological
and emotional realities of Bowery life and then emphasized the
muddled sentiments which mask those realities, here he dichot-
omizes the social structure of Fort Romper into two aspects that in-
teract and overlap in forming what might be defined as the Western
town in transition between the old and new West. The Palace Hotel
is new, but within it are preserved many devitalized forms of an
outdated culture. In contrast, the saloon, the foremost establish-
ment of older Western communities, operates in accord with the
reputable forms of the East. Together they breed violence which is
neither old nor new. Despite Scully's protestations and his priestly
role as host of a respectable hotel rife with civil ceremonies, his es-
tablishment is much like a hotel of the future, ostensibly civilized
West in which people act out roles not rightfully belonging to them.
The "tall bronzed cowboy"is a shadow of his authentic prototype;
while playing cards he is "a board-whacker." He is a man more of
talk than action, in many ways less the legendary Westerner than
the laconic "delicate" gambler of the saloon. The scene that greets
the Swede's entrance into the hotel is what one might expect on the
Nebraskan plains: a card game that "wore many names" is in full
flurry. Here the game is still called High-Five. The participants
quarrel, and one spits tobacco juice into a box of sawdust. An older
code of the West is invoked when the Swede cries out to Scully's
son, "You are cheatin'." The Swede, bolstered by Scully's offer of a
drink straight out of a bottle (tainted as a Western gesture by the
fact that the presence of women forces them to hide the bottle under
the bed), now feels that he has acclimatized himself to Western custom so that he is no longer a tenderfoot. He replaces the cowboy as

a board-whacker and mimics Western speech: "Well, old boy, that was a good square meal"; and in his accusation, he twangs out the word "cheatin'." In War Post the same accusation causes the gambler, Larpent, to shoot the accuser immediately; in Fort Romper, the ritual takes a milder form. Before the fist fight Scully assures the Swede in true Western manner that the fight is to be a fair showdown; "You'll not have to whip all of us." The men stick to the code, but their desires were like the stove in the hotel, "humming with godlike violence." The cowboy screams, "Kill him, Johnnie! Kill him! Kill him! Kill him!" and Scully, who once looked as if he were "going to flame out" over the Swede's posturing as a Westerner, finally bursts out that he would like to beat the Swede himself.

Convinced that he has triumphed by the code apparently shared with the inhabitants of the hotel, the Swede wanders into the saloon where he asserts, in mythic Western fashion, that the "bad night" and "weather" suit him fine, and offers to buy drinks for the bar. But the men drinking at a table do not operate by such Wild West amenities—at least not ostensibly. "Two were prominent local businessmen; one was the district-attorney; and one was a professional gambler of the kind known as 'square' . . . who led an exemplary home life." For all appearances, the Swede could have been in a saloon in Bayonne, New Jersey. Beneath this veneer of social respectability lies encapsulated in the gambler a truer remnant of the violent West than the Swede had bargained for. Soon he is dead, and only the gambler maintains anything resembling a Western facade, comfortable with his fate and secure in his isolation. In contrast, "the barkeeper was in the street dinning through the storm for help, and, moreover, companionship."

In later stories, Crane's indictment of the sham social values adopted by these Westerners who will abide a "wolf" as long as he is "mannerly" becomes intensely grim. In "Twelve O'Clock," concern for the form of law and order is explicitly linked to self-interest and appeasement of the "eastern capiterlist [sic]." Unwilling to tumble over himself to draw distinctions between East and West, Crane portrays these citizens as just as capable of erupting into irrational, anarchic violence as are the cowboys who invade the town.

In "Moonlight on the Snow," Larpent, whom Crane transforms into the devil, coldly cuts through the virtuous exclamations of War Post and exposes the reality of the boom-town West when he equates the gestures of civilization and justice to a "speculation in real estate." Larpent's detachment is extreme enough for him to cite his own proposed lynching as "an outing of real estate speculators." Crane closes "Twelve O'Clock," after a murder as chilling as one described by Isaac Babel, with "a curious grim silence" broken only by a clock: "little doors flew open, a tiny wooden bird appeared and cried 'Cuckoo'— twelve times." This is the final comment on the waste of life and on the inconsequence of those conflicting traditions, customs, and values presented in the story.

"The Blue Hotel" does not end in such mechanical, easily achieved cynicism, nor is the ending merely a gloss on what has preceded.[28] Rather, in providing another inconclusive point of view, it turns the story back on itself so that the reader is made aware of overlooked complicities in the Swede's death: complicities of character, such as the Easterner's consistent lack of commitment, evident even in his reluctance to assert whether he thinks the panicky visitor to be a Swede or a Dutchman; and complicities of social forms, such as the characters' conspiring to act according to a gambling code which, as the Easterner implies, has little relevance to the immediate situation. The Easterner concludes that the "poor" gambler, who eventually kills the Swede, "isn't even a noun" but "kind of an adverb." Even if the Easterner is only partially correct, the Swede himself is definitely a substantive. The Easterner's "fog of mysterious theory" is not untrue, but it is only one aspect of the truth. The prime agent and victim of this drama remains the Swede himself.

It is easy enough to trace the misperceptions and misconceptions that cause the Swede to conspire in the working out of his fate; yet he is not simply the victim of quixotic delusions and hallucinations. The Easterner reveals that Johnnie *was* cheating; paranoids, Delmore Schwartz reminds us, have real enemies too. "Oh, I see you are all against me," the Swede says to the men in the hotel; and they are. It might be said that the Swede makes the mistake of not respecting his initial "hallucinations." In "The Blue Hotel," "a thousand things might have happened"; but if the Swede had been as paranoid in the saloon as in the hotel, his fate might have been different. Without denying his original delusions, it is important to realize that his perception about Johnnie is true, and so in a sense is his hallucination about Scully, whose "wrinkled visage . . . resembled a murderer." Later, Scully tells the others, "Upstairs he thought I was tryin' to poison 'im." In a sense, he was; but the Swede, whose perceptions at first cause him to jerk "his hand away and cast a look of horror upon Scully," finally does drink from the bottle. His drinking poisons him into accepting Scully's Chamber of Commerce platitudes and into thinking that his aggressive role of Western bravado is an appropriate safeguard against danger. At one point Scully was about to react to the Swede's manner, but chose to mask his impulse with a silent, "sickly smile." "The others understood from his manner that he was admitting his responsibility for the Swede's new viewpoint." A short poem from *The Black Riders* applies as much to the Swede's original viewpoint as it does to the Western viewpoint maintained by the gambler, despite his having a "real wife and two real children in a neat cottage."

> A man feared that he might find an assassin;
> Another that he might find a victim.
> One was more wise than the other.   *[BR, 56]*

Little did the Swede know that were he wise enough originally to fear finding a victim, he might not have found his assassin. But the "if's" keep piling up in this "human movement." Nothing is certain. After all, it was "by chance" that the Swede laid his hand upon the shoulder of the gambler, the man whose knife would have flashed faster than Johnnie's fists at the cry, "You are cheatin'." Ironically, the Swede probably would have perceived no reason to voice that opinion while playing with the professional.

Compared to "The Blue Hotel," both "Twelve O'Clock" and "Moonlight on the Snow" schematically outline only a few components of Western life, and they in no way approach that story's psychological penetration or its devastating attack on social custom and conventional morality. Put the Palace Hotel and the saloon together and there develops a composite picture of the mixed and contradictory elements comprising both Western society and American society in general, in which the individual—at least the individual as represented in American fiction—has always been ill at ease. It is not only the Swede who is alienated in Fort Romper. Scully is acting out the role of an "honored an' respicted gintleman [sic]," and his identity is the result of sheer willful assertion. Fort Romper is a cruder town than he is willing to admit; even the "benevolence" and "small ceremonies" he extends toward cash-paying customers, whom he practically makes prisoners, cannot hide the fact that the basins he offers his guests are filled with "the coldest water in the world." The simple fact that Scully has been a resident of Fort Romper for fourteen years suggests that he is of a tougher breed than is indicated by his appearance, "curiously like an old priest," and by his speech, composed of various idioms and "scraps of curiously formal diction." Only once in the story do Scully's disguises become transparent; Western and formal idioms disappear, and as he speaks in his natural voice, his words express something other than priestly benevolence: "The old man burst into sudden brogue. 'I'd loike to take that Swade,' he wailed, 'and hould 'im down on a shtone flure and bate 'im to a jelly wid a shtick!' "

A veneer of social hypocrisy also exists in the saloon, where the prominent citizens cordially drink with the "thieving card player" because they are confident "he would never dare think of attacking their wisdom and courage." Moreover, the gambler is an exemplary citizen, always "so generous, so just, so moral" that it does not matter to anyone that he is "the wolf." What matters to the townsfolk is that it is not their lost money. More important are the uneasily maintained customs of the hotel and the saloon, which allow the men to function while the blizzard swirls around them but also blind them to their true predicament. In contrast, the Swede acquires a certain nobility in his failure to accommodate himself to the social conventions and phony social identities of either hotel or saloon. True to his own perceptions and to the code he thinks valid, the Swede whips Johnnie, and for a brief moment, the Easterner sees him as a man transformed:

There was a splendor of isolation in his situation at this time which
the Easterner felt once when, lifting his eyes from the man on the
ground, he beheld that mysterious and lonely figure, waiting.

[V, 161]

But the story ends in a dilemma. While Henry Fleming was lucky
enough to find an arbitrary construction of tradition that protected
him from the metaphysical horror he saw in an isolated corpse, the
Swede retains the "splendor of isolation" and becomes that cipher
himself. However capricious or false, the communal forms of the
saloon and hotel are necessities for survival. Outside of them, the
tragedy of existence is "accentuated by the long, mellow cry of the
blizzard." People, from this point of view, are no more than lice,
and one is a coxcomb not to die. Maggie did die. "However, the
Swede found a saloon" to protect him momentarily from the horror
of the storm; and yet within the saloon, as within the hotel, there is
another horror equally great. Human nature, like the stove in the
hotel, is always "humming with godlike violence. . . . The stove
was in midcurrent of the blast, and its voice swelled to equal the
roar of the storm." Throughout his career Crane had swept aside
the curtain of the commonplace and exposed the demonic nature
of existence—in storms, seas, fires, society, and that "composite
monster," war. In the Western tales he more clearly exposes the
demonic forces lurking in each individual, including the Swede
himself. "The Blue Hotel" reveals how the mythical Wild West
often became reality in unexpected places because its true locale
was a country in the mind.

❧ 5 ❧

THE LIMITS OF CRANE'S ARTISTRY

———•·•———

So strange had been the apparition of these men,
their dress had been so allied in color to the soil, their
passing had so little disturbed the solemn rumination
of the forest, and their going had been so like a
spectral dissolution, that a witness could have
wondered if he dreamed. THE CLAN OF NO-NAME

Crane's art is admittedly of narrow range. There is nothing of Melville's expansiveness in it, nor of James' ramifications of social encounter, nor of Whitman's multitudes. Yet such Sunday-book-review comparisons of range and bulk can do little justice to the startlingly intensive performance of a brief career. Conrad's cautious lament remains a more fitting consideration: "His grip is strong but while you feel the pressure on your flesh you slip out from his hand—much to your own surprise" (*Letters*, p. 156). We are surprised because Crane, as his friend says in the same letter, has strength, rapidity of action, an amazing faculty of vision, outline, color, movement—everything, in short, that an artist of staying power might have. Which brings up the larger and perhaps unanswerable question of what makes a work memorable, what qualities are necessary for that particular binding impress on the mind that causes a work to germinate long after the book is closed so that a reader's enthusiasm flares. Certainly Crane's characters,

even Maggie or Fleming, do not invade our memories as does an
Ahab, a Gatsby, or even a Wakefield or Rappaccini. And with a few
possible exceptions, such as Jim Conklin's dance of death, what
events in Crane's fiction return with the weight of historic development or dramatic vividness? Four men adrift at sea in an open
boat is potentially a situation of high drama, but in terms of remembered particulars, nothing much happens. We do remember pictures: Potter staring down Wilson, the Kid from New York staring
down the Mexican posed as a Spanish grandee, Fleming staring at a
corpse, the Swede at a cash register, Judge Hagenthorpe at a monster's unwinking eye, and Timothy Lean at an upturned face. Even
if specifics of character and event cannot be recalled (and generally
they can't—at least not commonly agreed-on specifics, for at their
most reductive they are only a bunch of words), from fiction that retains its grip there always remains a memory that the arrangement of
characters and events somehow formed a design that made sense,
that in a world without shape an order was realized. That order
need not return with the formal precision of a pictorial design or
a repeated theme in music—the work may even be "unfinished."
But the feeling remains that for once relations fell together according to some sensible human fiction, by which we would commonly
like to see our lives but which in honest moments we must admit
does not exist in the world around us, a world that goes on without
beginning or end, "a great calm thing rolling noiselessly toward
the end of the mystery" (V, 121).

As old-fashioned as these characteristics might appear now, they
are discoverable in most nineteenth-century fiction that has en-
dured through a renewable appeal to "the common reader," and
may indeed be part of what Conrad found wanting in Crane's
work. Yet these are the very virtues Crane rejected. Only when
pressed did he give the fictional figures in *Maggie* any names at all.
Reviewers criticized his lack of interest in events, but he continued
to write stories in which nothing happened. Unwilling to see relations between events as they were presumed by the fictional structures of his contemporaries, he became one of the early innovators
of the plotless story. While these self-imposed limitations insured a
loss to literature as readers generally knew it, they freed experience,

as Crane knew it, from the shackles of structural formulas. There
was a price to be paid, and according to the larger measure of
Conrad's judgment, Crane still disappoints. But these sacrifices en-
abled him to dramatize how fatuous is the immediate linkage of
identity to a name, social position, or action, allowing him to examine how a man first defines himself by a point of view. In Crane's
fiction a shift in point of view can be as important as a rifle bullet
through the thorax. Whether or not a situation evolves into an iden-
tifiable action is less crucial than are all the normally unseen components of potential action. Despite contrary appearances, Crane
shows that nothing is static; and human acts are never truly apprehended until they are broken into their components, and labels
disappear. An urgent assertion of usable patterns and forms in literature too eagerly diminishes to human terms a world that is limit-
lessly dynamic and random. Conclusions are not to be toyed with,
and even those Crane stories which masterfully employ accepted
narrative techniques, like "The Blue Hotel," finally elude normal
schematization through their emphasis upon the inconclusive.

> "Truth," said a traveller,
> "Is a breath, a wind,
> A shadow, a phantom;
> Long have I pursued it,
> But never have I touched
> The hem of its garment."   [BR, 28]

Crane's rejection of traditional techniques finds modern echoes in
"the tension or dissonance between paradigmatic form and contingent reality" that troubled Sartre, Musil, and other authors discussed by Frank Kermode in *The Sense of an Ending*. [1] These writers
maintain there is an inherent simplicity in narrative order that is
not shared by reality, and any easy adaptation of patterns, myths,
or philosophies that blinds us to the pure contingency of modern
reality is dishonest. The similarity to Crane's aesthetic attitude is
not surprising—H. G. Wells is not alone in dating Crane's work as
the beginning of modern American literature—but it is not necessary to propel Crane into the mid-twentieth century. The modern
call of "existential" artists for immediacy and sincerity, a call shared
by Crane as a "romantic" artist, and the modern rejection of "old

solemn art as being in *mauvaise foi"* substantiate Iris Murdoch's contention that existentialism is really "the last fling of liberal Romanticism in philosophy." The contemporary "happening," she says, shares these values and is therefore "the proper child of existentialism." [2] However, though they try to be sincere and immediate, true to a changed sense of reality, the works of Crane, Sartre, and Musil are not happenings. Crane, who shared Poe's stern sense of craft, was too aware of the chaos around him to let his work contribute to that chaos by duplicating pure contingency. Art is ceremony. Necessarily arbitrary, though not absolutely fraudulent, his art is a stay against the horror of the nothingness it delineates. Relations end nowhere, James reminds us, and every artist must finally draw his circle somewhere, no matter how wide the circumference. That geometric design is art, artifice—a violation of nature. Musil and Sartre, too, as Kermode observes, are forced to accept the *"a priori* limitations" of the novel, the inescapable fact that form is imposed by simply starting and stopping a literary work, and by providing it with potential for change.[3] Crane most successfully walks that thin line between the fraudulent and the meaningless in those short stories, such as "The Open Boat," whose open form least falsifies contingent reality.

It is in the organization of his longer, more episodic works that Crane seems to cause profoundest disappointment and most often loses his grip on the reader after the book is closed. Torn between a sense of the inconclusiveness of individual reflection and a desire for some realization of manhood on his character's part, Crane seems to have opted for neither in *The Red Badge*. The reader knows that somehow Fleming has become a member of his regiment, he is a veteran of sorts, but the statement "He was a man" (with Crane's special implications of that word) has never been substantiated to everyone's satisfaction in terms of the dramatic events of the novel. The reflective conclusions of the last chapter are too similar to those of chapter 15 for the former to be trustworthy. Whatever Crane's intentions, the unstated implications of the drama are not sufficiently precise for the reader to know whether Henry really is what he seems to be at the end of the novel. *Maggie* also is the product of an artistic sensibility not yet strong enough to accept the contradictions within itself and within its subject. Missing is the particular power of the artist, as opposed to that of the craftsman, the power to transcend conscience and to comprehend a fictional world as a whole, despite all its possible irregularities. The result is confusion rather than the clear ambivalence found in "The Open Boat" and "The Blue Hotel." Although an artist's ultimate subject may be mystery, he must not obscure that mystery through mystifications of his own. When Crane gave up the struggle of giving form to his uncommon perceptions, the results were *The Third Violet*, *Active Service*, and *The O'Ruddy*. Each has Crane's imprint; each— especially remarkably energetic portions of *The O'Ruddy*—entertains and excites our imaginations in flashes. But unlike the other novels, and even unlike *George's Mother* (which is half novel and half personal essay), none fundamentally affects our way of seeing the world around us.

The technical refusals and innovations Crane perpetrated in the name of sincerity bear the seeds of further artistic limitations that have become self-willed in the kind of "modern" novel that is "developing within itself those elements which will show how it is related to the rest of reality." [4] Despite Michel Butor's claims for this contemporary activity, there is really nothing astonishingly new about it. Crane's realization that there remains a gap between his own artifice and experience is commonly shared by earlier nineteenth-century romancers. Americans, it seems, have always been wary of their own fictional inventions, and the works of Hawthorne, Poe, Melville, and even James abound with indirect and direct commentary on the role of the artist and on the activity in which he is immediately engaged, as well as the relationship of that process to the rest of reality. At its most modern extreme, when literary process becomes the subject of itself, the author may lose the power to conquer a world larger than the vagaries of his own mind. In *The Man Without Qualities*, Robert Musil announces that "no serious attempt will be made to . . . enter into competition with reality." [5] If acted upon, a conviction that nothing true can be said about reality, or a reluctance to make up one's mind, can be self-defeating in its self-consciousness, confusion, and absence of illumination about anything at all.

Crane was not entirely free from the quandaries posed by such an incestuous relationship between the writer and his work. There is a distracting self-consciousness in his fiction, other than that written when he was merely being clever. "One Dash—Horses" is only one example. And his transfigurations of reality put him dangerously close to those nineteenth-century artists who, as Auerbach says, "consistently value life only as literary subject." [6] There are personal references in Crane's work that ultimately remain private, but to shuffle him off into the daisy land of Art-for-Art's sake is as condemnatory and as narrow as seeing him only as a proponent of Naturalism, for both, as W. H. Auden remarks, are "expressions of the same megalomania." The one kind of artist sees himself as the only "authentic human being," and his work as the "only true religion"; the other sees everyone and everything except himself and his work as "enslaved to necessity." [7] Both, according to Auden, originated from the nineteenth-century condition of the artist's finding himself a social oddity and thus alternating between feelings of guilt and superiority. Crane, who already considered himself stigmatized as a preacher's son was also that late nineteenth-century American phenomenon, the Writer. Never a surveyor in a customhouse, a sailor, or a minister before or while he wrote, he was without any other trade. Understandably he bears some of the impoverishing marks of the alienated aesthete as described by Auden and Auerbach, but ultimately, according to the defining terms of both critics, Crane escapes megalomania and exact categorization through his humor and irony.

Mordant as it may be at times, a comic sense suffuses his work. "Your little brother is neither braggart or a silent egotist," he wrote to William Crane (*Letters*, p. 147), and he was right, for he did not spare even himself from that wit that razed everything within its ken. Equally important, as Ralph Ellison has shown,[8] is the range of keen historical awareness informing all Crane's best work. The Western tales bring this awareness to the surface in their astute observations of social and historical process. Finally, Crane's conviction that "art is man's substitute for nature" (*Letters*, p. 31) is not an endorsement of withdrawal. Crane enters into direct competition with reality, an act, he knew, of folly and conceit, but also an expression of human vitality, for in flinging these ceremonial acts of fiction into timeless disorder, he momentarily "destroys the disorder and the dead time of the world." [9] The purpose of these substitutes is not to replace reality but to provide the means of getting "the nearest to nature and truth." Only by transforming nature, by making it strange, can we illuminate what is ordinarily imperceptible. [10] At this point, Crane the romantic joins hands with the existentialists of Kermode's study, for who is this illuminator, this transformer, this true hero, but the artist himself? Crane, as the seer, the man aware of his special sensibility, [11] the man courageous enough to accept the oddity of his position outside of normal society, the man who implies that the kind of sensibility registered in writing is the same sensibility necessary to savor experience, the man who can remain the "isolato" true to his perceptions and even his hallucinations without joining the Swede on a barroom floor— even when invisible, that man is the true hero at the core of all Crane's art. [12] When he did make himself highly visible, in his dispatches from Greece, Crane opened himself to what is the best of the many and often superficial parodies of his work. This anonymous piece from Maine was reprinted in the New York *Tribune* in 1897:

> I have seen a battle.
> I find it is very like what
> I wrote up before.
> I congratulate myself that
> I ever saw a battle.
> I am pleased with the sound of war.
> I think it is beautiful.
> I thought it would be.
> I am sure of my nose for battle.
> I did not see any war correspondents while
> I was watching the battle except
> I. [13]

That "I" is Crane's two-edged sword. Consistently present in even his most "objective" works, it is the source of his art's integrity. It is also most likely the first reason Conrad felt Crane's pressure, just as it is probably the reason he slipped from Crane's grasp, for that "I" is governed by the perceptions and voice of a poet. Not only are the techniques of "The Open Boat," as Daniel Hoffman contends, "essentially the techniques of poetry," [14] but the concentrated language of that story is the natural expression of an intensely subjective emotional response. Interest in human relations pales before Crane's interest in the individual's relationship to the universe; or rather, the point of view and voice in his work are those of a man acutely aware of that relationship, almost as if he himself were stationed in some sidereal void. The current running through his work is the lyric cry, and the reader is forced to speak of it metaphorically, as Mailer does in commenting on that "sense of a fire on the horizon which comes back always from *The Red Badge of Courage*," [15] or as Pritchett does when he says, "Crane starts a bugle call and sustains it without falter to the end of the book." [16] Whether in verse or prose, the virtue of Crane's art is found less in a work's structure than in the individual phrases that make up what is normally called its texture, and it is to texture that Conrad referred when he talked about "ideas" in Crane's fiction: "yours come out sharp cut as cameos—they come all living out of your brain and bring images—and bring light" (*Letters*, p. 167). In citing the effectiveness of a detail in *The Nigger of the Narcissus*, Crane was praising what he himself did best: "I felt ill over that red thread lining from the corner of the man's mouth to his chin. It was frightful with the weight of a real and present death. By such small means does the real writer suddenly flash out in the sky above those who are always doing rather well" (*Letters*, p. 150). With all Crane's best work, the reader must return to his exact phrasing. Memorable "characters" and "events," the creations of narrative or dramatic sequences, at times can maintain in our minds a reasonable though, perhaps, distorted life apart from their contexts. Like a lyric poem, a Crane story works in smaller units, and one must constantly return to the words and individual sentences that trace those elusive shiftings and turnings of consciousness, feeling, and sensibility.

The poetic impulse, as Crane's longer pieces show, does not easily adapt to the humdrum busywork of constructing houses of fiction. H. L. Mencken noted that Crane was weak in passage work— "he lacked the pedestrian talent for linking one thing to another" [17]—but Crane wasn't concerned with these novelistic contrivances. As in "An Eloquence of Grief," he wanted to get on to that girl's scream that "disclosed the gloom-shrouded spectre . . . in so universal a tone of the mind." There is something of the expressionist behind this impulse; the world of measurement often gets shoved aside in favor of some emotion-ridden realm that functions according to its own principles and ignores all common sense. As Larzer Ziff observed, "There simply isn't enough furniture and crockery in a habitation like that of the Johnsons to yield the supply necessary for the crunching destruction" [18] that goes on there. Emotions become larger and more real than characters or events. Although such creative projections may take their shape from an author's feelings, they may also float in a void when they fail to call enough attention to the causes of those feelings, or at least the amount of attention that fictional models of the world usually require. This limited specialness of vision and fictional invention seems to be the second fundamental reason Crane slips from our grasp; the realms he enters often bear only minimal relation to familiar experience.

If Crane was a poet, he was anything but a poet of the familiar. One must return to the phrasing of details not only for their qualification of incident, but for the quality of the details themselves. The distortions and transfigurations they effect will not adjust to a common-sense and a conventionally moral framework. In the world of "A Mystery of Heroism," a wounded horse turns its nose "with mystic and profound eloquence toward the sky," while an officer's eyes, resembling beads, sparkle "like those of an insane man." Collins finds his initial action "supernaturally strange." He "appeared as a man dreaming," and he "suddenly felt that two demon fingers were pressed into his ears. . . . The sky was full of fiends." Reaching the well, the expected source of relief from his heat and thirst, he discovers a "pink reflection" from "Crimson light" shining through "swift-boiling smoke," and jerks away from this "furnace." In this demonic realm there "screamed practical angels of death." Still, Collins ran away like a "farmer chased out of a dairy by a bull." Few novelists, Mailer claims, can move with ease "from mystical to practical reactions with [their] characters. . . . It's the hint of greatness." [19] When Collins sees his regiment, "his comrades were standing looking at him from the edge of an impossible star. He was aware of some deep wheelruts and hoofprints in the sod beneath his feet."

Because of his reluctance to remain earthbound, Crane found his most suitable subjects outside the continuum of daily life. A writer more "normal" and architectonic in presentation might look at an incident asking, "What will happen?" and then trace his deductions from observable circumstances.[20] The result might be a novel which creates an air of inevitability, persuading the reader that actions and scenes are necessary consequences of some initial situation. Crane, on the other hand, would not have been interested in questions such as what happens to particular men or what do they think when attending the funeral of a close friend. He would ask *what would happen if* this burial were held on a battlefield and the men themselves had to throw dirt on their friend's upturned face. The range of emotions, the customs and rituals, and the moral obligations that might be taken for granted in the first kind of storytelling are thus called into question. Such a story creates the oblique vision, the unique scene Crane was after, and it qualifies preconceived notions, but the effects might slip away once a reader closes the book and readjusts his frame of reference. The stories become even more slippery when the experiences described become rarer than the situations in which they occur. Certainly this is true of Fleming and Collins when they approach a mystic's clarity of vision. Combined with the other charged and even transcendental moments occurring in unusual circumstances, these stories give support to Poe's statement, "All high excitements are necessarily transient."[21] In compensation, Crane often freezes time, strips it of a past and future, and anatomizes an event into particulars; but such an act may be too great a negation of a reader's sense that reality is also motion. If it is to be seen with fidelity to life as experienced, a reader might say, a moment must depend upon time as well as upon intensity of feeling or sensation. But Crane concentrated on the latter, and the effect of his words depends largely on their immediate impact on the reader, since he is not only a describer but, as Harold Martin has said, an "exciter."[22] The purposeful arousal of intense feeling or sensation is extreme in Crane's

ness . . . as some sugar-snow in March" (p. 15). A Negro's face "glowed like a polished copper saucepan" (p. 27), while a miser's was a "wizened apple upon a grimy snow-bank" (p. 90). And the entire movement of the opening chapter possesses the silence and symbolic autonomy of a dream. Similarly, Emily Dickinson, aware that "Perception of an object costs / Precise the Object's loss," [31] transforms objects so that they might properly be apprehended. The special significance of an object or moment requires a gradual movement from the literal until, as in her description of a bird, it is entirely abandoned:

> And he unrolled his feathers
> And rowed him softer home—
>
> Than Oars divide the Ocean,
> Too silver for a seam—
> Or Butterflies, off Banks of Noon
> Leap, plashless as they swim. [32]

A special significance of Crane's kind of visionary expression is that it opens up to the reader a view of the world diametrically opposed to the public American view of the 1890s. As Ralph Ellison has said, "Now there was much of which Americans were morally aware but little which they wished to confront in literature, and the compelling of such confrontation was the challenge flung down to Crane by history." [33] Not in his themes and subjects alone, but in his words and their arrangement, Crane produced works that became his way of nose-thumbing a romance-reading public, his antiface to the national dream of progressive America, or to borrow a phrase, they became his NO! in thunder to all the world's yea-sayers—"if for nothing else," as Melville once said of such denials, "than as a counterpoise to the exorbitant hopefulness, juvenile and shallow, that makes such a bluster in these days." [34] Crane found hope to be the most vacuous of emotions, for it usually stems from a failure of perception that denies man's limitations by making man into a kind of god who can view the world and its problems objectively as apart from himself. The antagonist of Crane's consistent mode of transfiguring perception—the fusing of inner and outer experience—is that frame of mind which degrades all mysteries into solvable problems. The implication of Crane's prose is that the difficulty with a hopeful problem-solving approach to mystery is that the solver tends to exclude himself from the "problem" of which he is a part. He tends to look on something like evil as a disorder outside of himself, rather than seeing that his own position as both problem and solver makes his relationship to the universe one of mystery. Crane diverts both his readers and himself from packaging the mysteries of reality, he prevents singleness of vision by insuring multiple perspectives. Crane's refusal to systematize makes it almost impossible for the reader to cast judgment without also implicating himself. More importantly, this sort of imaginative activity, which bears a close resemblance to the associative logic of dreams, implicates the man doing the imagining, just as the dream implicates the dreamer.

A view of Crane in the context of his age as a "modern" American innovator gives public validity to many of those habits of style and method that are too quickly seen as reflections of some private bias—his acclaimed tendency, for instance, to degrade man, to dehumanize and depersonalize him. When his stylistic and methodological habits are accepted not as personal aberrations but as vision itself, then there is no way of seeing, as Jane Mayhall has said, any "forced or gratuitous difference between what he observed and what he said." [35] Crane, with his special interest in individual integrity, saw the struggle of the individual against the depersonalizing forces of a society formed in an age of progress. He saw the process of isolation and dehumanization taking shape in the newer society of the West as well as in the older one of New York, an effect caused as much by a certain frame of mind and misplaced values as by environment and "the system." War served as the ideal metaphor as well as the extreme literal realization of a developing world in which men were "closer to machines than humans." [36] and machines were closer to men. Even in "The Pace of Youth," Stimson is a less animate character than is his giant machine, the merry-go-round. Crane established a perceptual framework that informed later novels and became overt themes of those coming out of World War II, from The Naked and the Dead to Catch-22, in which there is an emphasis on the animation of the inert, the deanimation of the human, and the erosion of meaning and integrity from human feelings and impulse.

The nervous, dynamic, often fairy-tale world of Crane's fiction indeed seems the product of a primitive, childlike vision, but as Dorothy Van Ghent says of Dickens's similarly demonically motivated world, "if people turn themselves or are turned into things, metaphysical order can be established only if we think of things turning themselves into people, acting under a 'dark' drive similar to that which motivates the human aberration." [37] As with Dickens, Crane's persistent use of the pathetic fallacy becomes more than stylistic embellishment through his equally insistent employment of a reciprocal metaphor in his descriptions of people. In "A Mystery of Heroism," it is the guns that have "demeanors of stolidity and courage," while the men appear as "a part of the clay bank which shielded them from the shells." A world in which occult and demonic forces move in and out of things and people is best represented through abrupt hallucinatory details. Images overlap, details of the most ordinary perceptions fuse with images of man's deepest obsessions and fears. A cartridge belt becomes the arms of a dead man to Peza, his rifle a snake. George Kelcey, who has ceased to be human through his drinking, becomes reduced to what he might perceive during delirium tremens: "Kelcey began to stare at the wallpaper. The pattern was clusters of brown roses. He felt them like hideous crabs crawling upon his brain" (I, 178). Kelcey becomes like the "you" in Eliot's "Preludes," reduced to what you see flickering against the ceiling, "The thousand sordid images / Of which your soul was constituted." [38] Since Eliot's time, Crane's vision of reciprocal change has become deeply ingrained in the consciousness of contemporary artists. In *Of a Fire on the Moon*, Norman Mailer seems to find the technicians, engineers, and astronauts, all those responsible for the first moon shot, so bureaucratized, programmed, computerized, and sterilized, so lacking in personality, sensuality, and distinctive psychological complexity, that Saturn V becomes the true hero of the book, and the most heroic acts are those of the rocket, beginning with its apocalyptic blastoff. In his efforts to create some metaphysical order in this technological void, Mailer ends up creating a demonically mo-

tivated world, and devotes fifty-five pages of his book to an investigation of "The Psychology of Machines."

Not quite as inverted as Mailer's world of space exploration,
Crane's fictional world of war and adventure left room for man to
find individual expression through fine deeds and defiant gestures.
Crane apparently tested his own mettle through frequent exposures
to rifle fire during the Cuban War. We become what we sing,
Matthew Arnold remarked, and Crane's imitations of both stance
and action deemed honorable by his fiction earned for him Richard
Harding Davis's tribute that he was "the coolest man, whether
army officer or civilian, that I saw under fire at any time during the
war." [39] The judgment is external, and one can only wonder how
closely Crane approached that visionary point of view shared by the
correspondent in the open boat, Collins, and Fleming when, totally
depersonalized, they viewed a scene as though in a gallery, and
every detail was made clear to them except why they themselves
were there. One observer, watching Crane light a cigarette while
"bullets hissed past him into the mud," declared that it "was impossible . . . to question the insouciance of this act: Crane's bearing was that of a somnambulist. He appeared to be, as it were, detached from himself, possessed by an irresistible impulse to
register, in his body, and without regard to the safety of his body,
certain sensations." [40] As Crane demonstrated in his fiction, there
is no way for an observer to judge the true merits of an apparent
battle sleep. A man may be the embodiment of fear or its very opposite—at that moment, devoid of self-consciousness, he may be
most intensely and perfectly himself, viewing the world in its keenest perspective. Of course, he may simultaneously be like the
Swede, seeking his own death, or like the correspondent, merely
indifferent to it.

In presenting an event of uncommon significance Crane did not
rely on a scheme of conventional morality or common sense, nor
did he gain satisfaction in solely probing into the complexities of
some deeper psychology. He went beyond the rim of normal perception and transformed the truly significant into the color and
form of certain apparitional moments, which by their nature are
inevitably intense, fleeting, radiant, sometimes dreadful, some-

times splendid, always awesome. This activity of mental light and shade can transfigure even the most trivial of scenes. In *The Red Badge*, Crane portrayed the demonic nature of war through "occasional glimpses of visages that loomed pallid and ghostly, lit with a phosphorescent glow" (*RB*, 257), and two years before the Cuban War, he described how the "fog made the clothes of the column of men in the roadway seem of a luminous quality. It imparted to the heavy infantry coats a new color . . ." (VI, 3). Much the same might have happened at the Battle of San Juan, which "was like Inkerman," Crane reported, "where the English fought half leaderless all day in a fog. Only the Cuban forest was worse than any fog" (IX, 155). During that battle, while under excessively heavy fire, Crane again stood up and walked about; but that action is less haunting than is an imaginary snapshot of how Crane might have looked, for, as Davis reported, Crane was dressed in white. "He wore a long rain-coat and, as he stood peering over the edge of the hill with his hands in his pockets and smoking his pipe, he was as unconcerned as though he were gazing at a cinematograph." [41] Two years later he was dead, but to the very end, it was as if Crane were testing the authenticity of his strange world, and all the time, it seems, he was becoming more of what he sang.

NOTES

PREFACE

[1] O'Faoláin, *The Short Story*, p. 11.

[2] "Introduction," *The Works of Stephen Crane*, ed. Bowers (University Press of Virginia edition), VII, xiii–xiv. Subsequent references to the Virginia edition will be noted by volume and page number in the text.

[3] Berryman, *Stephen Crane*, p. 268.

[4] *The Red Badge of Courage* in *The Complete Novels of Stephen Crane*, ed. Gullason, p. 240. Gullason's edition has been chosen as text for *The Red Badge*, hereafter cited in the text as *RB*.

[5] "Introduction," *The Work of Stephen Crane*, ed. Follett, X, x.

[6] *Stephen Crane: Letters*, ed. Stallman and Gilkes, p. 156. Hereafter cited as *Letters*.

[7] Frank Norris, *Wave*, 4 July 1896, p. 13.

[8] LaFrance, *A Reading of Stephen Crane*, p. 59.

[9] Ibid., p. 64.

[10] Norris, *Wave*, 4 July 1896, p. 13.

[11] For Crane's use of this phrase, see Linson, *My Stephen Crane*, p. 32, and "War Memories" in *Works* (Virginia), VI, 222.

[12] Quoted in Ford Madox Ford, "Stevie and Company," *New York Herald Tribune Book Supplement*, 2 Jan. 1927, p. 6. According to Ford, James "constantly alluded to Crane as 'that genius,' and I have heard him say over and over again, 'He has great, great genius.' "

CHAPTER 1. VOICES OF PERCEPTION: CRANE'S PROSE STYLE

[1] A. J. Liebling, "The Dollars Damned Him," *The New Yorker*, 5 Aug. 1961, p. 66.

[2] Berryman, *Stephen Crane*, p. 284.

[3] See Thomas A. Gullason, "The Significance of *Wounds in the Rain*," *Modern Fiction Studies*, 5 (Autumn 1959), 235–42. Gullason maintains that in the later stories Crane's "style changed for the better. . . . His writing gained in depth: his style was no longer obtrusive." This contention is, of course, generally true, but Gullason's choice of passages for comparison is unfortunate. The section from "The Price of the Harness" contains moments when Crane lapses into simple hero-

worshiping statements presented in unexceptional prose: "There was something distinctive in the way they carried their rifles. There was the grace of an old hunter somewhere in it, the grace of a man whose rifle has become absolutely a part of himself. Furthermore almost every blue shirtsleeve was rolled to the elbow, disclosing forearms of almost incredible brawn. The rifles seemed light, almost fragile, in the hands that were at the end of those arms, never fat, but always rolling with muscles and veins that seemed on the point of bursting." In contrast, the passage from *The Red Badge* which Gullason disparages, though excessive, is particular, psychologically astute, morally investigatory, and sensually vivid (*RB*, 225–26). The observations of the above passage could be almost anyone's; those from *The Red Badge* could be only those of an artist.

4 Gordon, *How to Read a Novel*, p. 97.

5 Bridgman, *Colloquial Style*, p. 105.

6 Harold Martin, "The Development of Style in Nineteenth-Century American Fiction," *Style in Prose Fiction*, pp. 114–41.

7 Bridgman, *Colloquial Style*, p. 12.

8 Quoted in Read, *English Prose Style*, p. 154.

9 Twain, *A Tramp Abroad*, in *The Works of Mark Twain*, ed. Paine, X, Appendix D, 281.

10 See Øverland, "The Impressionism of Stephen Crane," in *Americana Norvegica*, ed. Skard and Wasser, I, 239–85. Øverland isolates this stylistic trait (p. 280), as well as some others mentioned later, for the purpose of showing that Crane's methods were essentially those of "impressionism," as that concept has been defined by various theoreticians.

11 "Maggie went away" is not only a stage direction but a thematic statement indicating Maggie's response to Pete's cry, "Oh, go t'hell!"

12 "Introduction," *The Work of Stephen Crane*, ed. Follett, IX, x–xi.

13 The electric chair at Sing Sing is made awful in a similar way: "But an odor of oiled woods, a keeper's tranquil, unemotional voice, a broom stood in the corner near the door, a blue sky and a bit of moving green tree at a window so small that it might have been made by a canister shot—all these ordinary things contribute with subtle meanings to the horror of this comfortable chair, this commonplace bit of furniture that waits in silence and loneliness, and waits and waits and waits.

"It is patient—patient as time. Even should its next stained and sallow prince be now a baby, playing with alphabet blocks near his mother's feet, this chair will wait. It is as unknown to his eye as are the shadows of trees at night, and yet it towers over him, monstrous, implacable, infernal, his fate—this patient, comfortable chair" (VIII, 665–66).

14 Kipling, *The Light That Failed*, in *Writings*, IX, 30–31.

15 Pritchett, "Two Writers and Modern War," *The Living Novel*, p. 173.

16 For other examples of this procedure, see Ziff, "Outstripping the Event: Stephen Crane," *The American 1890s*, p. 198.

17 Perosa, "Naturalism and Impressionism in Stephen Crane's Fiction," in *Stephen Crane: a Collection of Critical Essays*, ed. Bassan, p. 88.

[18] Kipling, *Writings*, IX, 40.

[19] Such sentences are less obtrusive in Crane's mature work, but even in a piece as late as "The Kicking Twelfth" (1900), they are again merely clever in the sense that they are ends in themselves. "He was almost the last man in the charge but not to his shame, rather to his stumpy legs" (VI, 295). Or, "If a man can put in long service with a mule battery and come out of it with an amiable disposition, he should be presented with a medal weighing many ounces" (VI, 291–92). One can almost hear Kipling, "The Soudan campaign and Dick's broken head had been some months ended and mended" (Kipling, *Writings*, IX, 34).

[20] See Harold Martin, "Development of Style," p. 132: "The preceding sentence is of equal interest because of the word *bath-tub*. To begin with, the image is unexpected and incongruous; in 1898 it was indecorous as well. (Is it not the word that one of James' heroes never mentions as the source of his income?)"

[21] The observation is Caroline Gordon's in *The House of Fiction*, ed. Gordon and Tate, p. 311.

[22] "Gass, "The Concept of Character in Fiction," *Fiction and the Figures of Life*, p. 44.

[23] "Introduction," *The Work of Stephen Crane*, ed. Follett, IX, xi.

[24] Philip Rahv, "Fiction and the Criticism of Fiction," *Kenyon Review*, 18 (1956), 280.

[25] Ibid., p. 180.

[26] "Introduction," *Sullivan County Sketches*, ed. Schoberlin, p. 13.

[27] For discussions and Howells's example of Crane's poetry written as prose, see W. D. Howells, "Life and Letters," *Harper's Weekly*, 25 Jan. 1896, p. 79, and Waggoner, *American Poets*, pp. 243–44.

[28] Ruth Miller, "Regions of Snow: The Poetic Style of Stephen Crane," *Bulletin of the New York Public Library*, 72 (1968), 329.

[29] *The Poems of Stephen Crane: A Critical Edition*, ed. Katz (rev. ed., 1971), poems numbered 130, 89, 113, and 67. Subsequent references to this edition will be identified by the letters *BR* (*The Black Riders*), *WK* (*War Is Kind*), *U* (Uncollected Poems), *PPP* (Posthumously Published Poems) and the number of the poem.

[30] See Ruth Miller, "Regions of Snow," pp. 338–41.

[31] A major exception is "A man adrift on a slim spar" (PPP, 113).

[32] Hoffman, *Poetry*.

[33] Arthur Oliver, "Jersey Memories—Stephen Crane," *New Jersey Historical Society Proceedings*, n.s. 16 (Oct. 1931), 455.

[34] Ruth Miller, "Regions of Snow," p. 349.

[35] For example: "a fat, stupid ass / Grinned at him from a green place" (*BR*, 55); or "Walking in the sky, / A man in strange black garb / Encountered a radiant form" (*BR*, 59); or "Many red devils ran from my heart / And out upon the page" (*BR*, 46).

[36] Øverland, "Impressionism," pp. 264–65, uses these sentences to demonstrate Crane's method of "stressing the importance of the individual impression of reality."

[37] Auerbach, *Mimesis,* p. 486.

[38] The misplaced subjective evaluation of the word *responsible* in "some blue police-man . . . beat the soft noses of the responsible horses" (I, 22) introduces a second (the man's) distorted point of view to a seemingly objective observation.

CHAPTER 2. CRANE'S HABIT OF IMAGINATION

[1] Hoffman, *Poetry,* p. 268.

[2] Hemingway, *Death in the Afternoon,* p. 2.

[3] Quoted in Auden, *A Certain World,* p. vii.

[4] Cather, "When I Knew Stephen Crane," in Bassan, ed., *Stephen Crane,* p. 16.

[5] For an account of Cather as an unreliable reporter, particularly in relation to Crane, see Woodress, *Willa Cather,* p. 66.

[6] A. J. Liebling, "The Dollars Damned Him," *The New Yorker,* 5 Aug. 1961, p. 66.

[7] Cather, "When I Knew Stephen Crane," p. 16.

[8] Quoted in Berryman, *Stephen Crane,* pp. 6, 256.

[9] See prologue in the Virginia edition, VIII, 862–63. Since most of Crane's stories are so short, specific page reference will be made only in those cases where the title of the work is not clearly indicated in the text, if the source is other than the Virginia edition, or if the quotation is long and separated from the text.

[10] Crane applies these methods of deformation in stories where they might not be expected, such as "The Pace of Youth," in which he presents scenes of young love from an uncommon perspective. To an ordinary observer, the youngsters in this drama would perhaps appear as the dullest things in a colorful seaside resort alive with bright lights, gay music, and "a great crowd intermingling, intertwining, sometimes colliding." Contrary to what might be expected from this kind of story, it is not the youngsters' romance, but the surrounding dazzle, whirl, and gaiety of the resort, delicately presented through sensory and suggestive means, that give the story its lilt. Instead of having to pump up a trite romance with an effulgence of emotional gush, Crane can use this bright world to suggest with a minimum of statement the uncommon splendor of the romance. In contrast to this "huge im-material background," the youngsters' common gestures and emotions acquire so-lidity and admirable strength. Finally, though, the triumph of their relationship occurs when, in contrast to their exciting happiness, a "fairy scene of the night" appears to be "phlegmatic and stolid." As with *Maggie,* Crane's method once again rescues a banal story from sentimentality by viewing it apart from the nor-mal perspectives and proportions of common sense.

[11] Berryman, *Stephen Crane,* p. 257.

[12] See Stallman, *Stephen Crane: A Biography,* pp. 244, 589. Before the *Commodore* in-cident Crane wrote of shipwrecks in "The Raft Story," "The Captain," "The Wreck of the New Era," "The Ghostly Spirit of Metedeconk," and "The Reluctant Voy-agers."

[13] Quoted in Berryman, *Stephen Crane,* pp. 6, 256.

14 Crane's fiction makes consistent use of gaslights, fierce little stoves, lighted windows, campfires for their eerie effects; these common objects become white radiances and lightning flashes in the poetry. The purpose is often merely transformative, a throwing of a peculiar strange light on a commonplace scene: "The gaslight that came with an effect of difficulty through the dust-stained windows on either side of the door, gave strange hues to the faces and forms of the three women who stood gabbling in the hall-way of the tenement" (VIII, 77). Light can often work as if on a stage or in a movie, emphasizing some incipient drama: "For, according to some mystic process, the smouldering coals of the fire went a-flame with sudden, fierce brilliance, splashing parts of the walls, the floor, the crude furniture, with a hue of blood-red. And in this dramatic out-burst of light, the girl saw her father seated at a table with his back turned toward her" (VIII, 79). Besides tone and transfiguration, the blood-red hue foreshadows the kind of discovery made in its light, for the girl soon sees that her father is dead. The same purpose of foreboding is found in "The Blue Hotel" as the Swede approaches the saloon where he is to be killed. "In front of it an indomitable red light was burning, and the snow-flakes were made blood-color as they flew through the circumscribed territory of the lamp's shining" (V, 165). All these examples substantiate Crane's penchant for the spectacular, the hallucinatory, the visionary.

15 For evidence that the sketch was a hoax, see Levenson, *Works* (Virginia), VII, xxii, and *New York City Sketches*, ed. Stallman and Hagemann, p. 43.

16 Michael Arlen, "Notes on the New Journalism," *Atlantic*, March 1972, p. 47.

17 See similar transformations throughout *The Red Badge*: "From this little distance the many fires, with the black forms of men passing to and fro before the crimson rays, made weird and satanic effects" (*RB*, 212).

18 See Berryman, *Stephen Crane*, p. 280; James B. Colvert, "Structure and Theme in Stephen Crane's Fiction," *Modern Fiction Studies*, 5 (Autumn 1959), 202–7; Holton, *Cylinder of Vision*, pp. 16, 42; Levenson, *Works* (Virginia), V, xvi–xvii; Jay Martin, *Harvests of Change*, pp. 64–65; and Solomon, *Parody*, pp. 4–18.

19 Berryman, *Stephen Crane*, p. 280.

20 Stallman, *Biography*, p. 10.

21 See Ford Madox Ford, "Henry James, Stephen Crane and the Main Stream," in *Thus to Revisit*, pp. 107–8; and *Letters*, p. 154, n. 127.

22 Crane told Willa Cather, "What I can't do, I can't do at all, and I can't acquire it. I only hold one trump." Cather, "When I Knew Stephen Crane," p. 15.

23 Berryman, *Stephen Crane*, p. 270.

24 Ruth Miller, "Regions of Snow: The Poetic Style of Stephen Crane," *Bulletin of the New York Public Library*, 72 (1968), 340–43.

25 Berthoff, *Ferment of Realism*, p. 233, 234.

26 When Crane does equate his bizarre or mesmerizing lines to some abstraction such as love or sin in "I explain the silvered passing of a ship at night" (*WK*, 81) and "Black Riders came from the sea" (*BR*, 1), the poems go limp, for as Berthoff remarks about "Black Riders," there is "a setting out of autonomous images which

the inert closing line of this first poem ('Thus the ride of sin') simply has no necessary contact with" (ibid., p. 234). Likewise, what remains in the mind from a
reading of "On the desert" is not that "The glory of slavery, despair, death/Is in
the dance of the whispering snakes," but rather the snakes themselves and the
other strange inhabitants of the desert:

> The whispering, whispering snakes
> Dreaming and swaying and staring
> But always whispering, softly whispering.
> The wind streams from the lone reaches
> Of Arabia, solemn with night,
> And the wild fire makes shimmer of blood
> Over the robes of the hooded men
> Squat and dumb.   [WK, 86]

27 See Øverland, "The Impressionism of Stephen Crane," in *Americana Nor-*
vegica, ed. Skard and Wasser, pp. 276–77.

28 James B. Colvert, "Structure and Theme in Stephen Crane's Fiction," *Modern Fic-*
tion Studies, 5 (Autumn 1959), 200.

29 See Crane's "A Lovely Jag in a Crowded Car." Certainly Crane sympathizes with
the deluded drunk rather than those "women who sat in austere silence regarding
each other in occasional furtive glances and preserving their respectability with
fierce vigilance," and certainly it is a delightful moment when the gentle drunk
destroys the atmosphere of the car, which "was as decorous as that of the most
frigid of drawing rooms" (VIII, 361).

30 Rourke, *American Humor,* pp. 62, 68.

31 Ibid., pp. 57–58.

32 Ibid., p. 49.

33 In "The Mesmeric Mountain," curiosity drives the little man to investigate a path
in the forest, quite "sure it leads to something great or something"; he feels certain he will make "some discovery or something"; but the path is exactly as described by a comrade, merely a road to Jim Boyd's place. The emotional high point
of the story, though, is not this discovery, but the description of Jones's mountain
as the little man experiences it in his anxious state; the mountain has eyes and
approaches him.

34 "These sounds . . . described the tremendous width of the stage of the prospec-
tive drama" (VI, 3), "The babe sat on the floor watching the scene, his face in con-
tortions like that of a woman at a tragedy" (I, 12). "The guns far and near were
roaring a fearful and grand introduction for this column which was marching upon
the stage of death" (VI, 7).

35 Other examples can be found throughout Crane's work. "Crimson serapes in the
distance resembled drops of blood on the great cloth of plain" (V, 22). Crane
writes that a firing line of rifles "reminds one always of a loom, a great grand steel
loom, clinking, clanking, plunking, plinking, to weave a woof of thin red threads,
the cloth of death" (VI, 109). In "A Fishing Village," the metaphor becomes more
elaborate: "Far to the south, where the slate of the sea and the grey of the sky
wove together, could be seen Fastnet Rock, a mere button on the moving, shim-

mering cloth, while a liner, no larger than a needle, spun a thread of smoke aslant" (VIII, 492).

36 "Introduction," *Work,* ed. Follett, VI, xix.

37 Berryman, *Stephen Crane,* p. 243.

38 Gass, "Even if, by All the Oxen in the World," *Fiction,* p. 269.

39 See Taylor, "The Laws of Life: Stephen Crane," *The Passages of Thought,* pp. 130–31. The moment occurs in chapter 19 of *The Red Badge* (*RB,* 277).

40 Mailer, *Cannibals and Christians,* p. 113.

41 See Conrad, "Stephen Crane," in *Last Essays,* p. 103.

42 Mark Schorer, "Technique as Discovery," *The Hudson Review,* 1 (Spring 1948), 84.

CHAPTER 3. CRANE'S SENSE OF STORY

1 O'Faoláin, *The Short Story,* p. 57.

2 Hartwick, *Foreground of American Fiction,* p. 42.

3 H. G. Wells, "Stephen Crane from an English Standpoint," *North American Review,* 171 (Aug. 1900), 242.

4 Quoted in Katz, ed., *The Portable Stephen Crane,* p. ix.

5 See O'Faoláin, *The Short Story,* pp. 153–54.

6 Quoted without reference in Stallman, ed., *Stephen Crane: An Omnibus,* p. 190.

7 Quoted in Ellen Moers, "When New York Made It," *New York Times Book Review,* 16 May 1971, p. 32.

8 *Maggie: A Girl of the Streets . . . A Facsimile Reproduction of the 1893 Edition,* ed. Katz, pp. 149, 143, and 144. For this discussion of the novel proper, the original *Maggie* has been chosen over the 1896 revision. For a defense of the 1893 *Maggie* as authorized text, see Joseph Katz, "The *Maggie* Nobody Knows," *Modern Fiction Studies,* 12 (Summer 1966), 200–12. The new Virginia edition poses new problems which Donald Pizer summarizes in his bibliographic essay on Crane. Pizer says that editor Fredson "Bowers's desire to achieve a single eclectic text results in a futile coalescing of two distinctive works—the 1893 *Maggie* and its 1896 revision—into what can only be called the Bowers *Maggie*." Pizer, "Stephen Crane," in *Fifteen American Authors before 1900,* ed. Rees and Harbert, p. 100. Hereafter cited as *Bibliography.* Subsequent page refrences to *Maggie* in this chapter are to the facsimile edition.

9 Charles Rosen, "Love That Mozart," *The New York Review of Books,* 18 May 1972, p. 16.

10 See Berryman, *Stephen Crane,* p. 58: "No American work of its length had driven the reader so hard."

11 See Joseph X. Brennan, "Ironic and Symbolic Structure in Crane's *Maggie,*" *Nineteenth-Century Fiction,* 16 (March 1962), 303–15; and Janet Overmyer, "The Structure of Crane's *Maggie,*" *University of Kansas City Review,* 29 (Autumn 1962), 71–72.

12 See Pizer, *Bibliography,* pp. 121–22: "The aspect of *Maggie* which has received the least satisfactory criticism is its form. . . . In short, as in criticism of *The Red*

Badge, though many writers approach the theme of *Maggie* through its form, few have attempted a full formalistic description or analysis of the novel."

[13] Forster, *Aspects of the Novel*, p. 130.

[14] See David Fitelson, "Stephen Crane's *Maggie* and Darwinism," *American Quarterly* 16 (Summer 1964), 182–84; Parrington, *Main Currents in American Thought*, III, 328–29; and Walcutt, *American Literary Naturalism*, p. 62–72.

[15] Reprinted as *The Night Side of New York Life;* p. 43.

[16] See Marcus Cunliffe, "Stephen Crane and the American Background of *Maggie*," *American Quarterly*, 7 (Spring 1955), 37: "At any rate, it presents Maggie as an experienced prostitute, who has apparently overcome her initial scruples. Moreover, she seems to have been reasonably successful, since she is wearing a 'handsome cloak' and has 'well-shod feet.' Why, then, does she commit suicide?" See also p. 41.

[17] Solomon, *Stephen Crane: From Parody to Realism*, p. 35 (hereafter cited as *Parody*); Cady, *Stephen Crane*, p. 104.

[18] See Holton, *Cylinder of Vision*, p. 43. Unlike other critics, Holton has noticed this simple division of "rude [sic] symmetry in the novel."

[19] General criticism of the dialogue in *Maggie* states that the characters make only verbal pronouncements without communicating. Despite its particular manifestations, this aspect of the dialogue, at least in the first half of the novel, may reflect the spirit of actual Bowery talk. See Edmund Leach, "Mythical Inequalities," *New York Review of Books*, 28 Jan. 1971, p. 44: "As a restricted code, which tends to be characteristic of working-class homes in which the parents have only limited educational equipment, language is a device which constantly reinforces the speaker's ideas about his own position in the total structure of society."

[20] Shattuck, *The Banquet Years* (rev. ed., 1968), p. 342.

[21] José Ortega y Gassett, "The Nature of the Novel," *The Hudson Review*, 10 (Spring 1957), 29.

[22] As noted earlier, all page references to *The Red Badge* are to Gullason, ed., *The Complete Novels of Stephen Crane*, pp. 197–299.

[23] Cazemajou, *Stephen Crane*, p. 19.

[24] See LaFrance, *A Reading of Stephen Crane*, pp. 120–24: "I am unable to find much irony in the closing paragraphs of the novel. . . . Henry has attained authentic self-knowledge and a sense of manhood after long and fierce battles with his own moral weakness." See R. B. Sewall, "Crane's *The Red Badge of Courage*," *Explicator*, 3 (May 1945), Item 55; John E. Hart, "*The Red Badge of Courage* as Myth and Symbol," *University of Kansas City Review*, 19 (Summer 1953), 249–56, and R. W. Stallman, "Notes Toward an Analysis of *The Red Badge of Courage*," in Bradley, Beatty, and Long, eds., *The Red Badge of Courage* (Norton Critical ed.), pp. 248–54.

Among those inclined to see the ending as ironic are Walcutt, *American Literary Naturalism*, pp. 66–86, Jay Martin, *Harvests of Change*, pp. 64–65, and Clark Griffith, "The Ironic Last Word," *Philological Quarterly*, 47 (Jan. 1968), 88–90.

Among those who see the presentation of Henry's development as ambiguous, ambivalent, or confused are Stanley B. Greenfield, "The Unmistakable Stephen

Crane," *PMLA*, 73 (1958), 562–72; James T. Cox, "The Imagery of *The Red Badge of Courage*," *Modern Fiction Studies*, 5 (Autumn 1959), 209–19; John W. Rathbun, "Structure and Meaning in *The Red Badge of Courage*," *Ball State University Forum*, 10 (Winter 1969), 8–16, Mordecai Marcus, "The Unity of *The Red Badge of Courage*," in Lettis, McDonnell, and Morris, eds., *Stephen Crane's* The Red Badge of Courage, pp. 189–95; and James B. Colvert, "Stephen Crane's Magic Mountain," in Bassan, *Stephen Crane*, pp. 95–105.

[25] Herman Melville writes: "But the mingled, mingling threads of life are woven by warp and woof: calms crossed by storms, a storm for every calm. There is no steady unretracing progress in this life; we do not advance through . . . infancy's unconscious spell, boyhood's thoughtless faith, adolescence' doubt (the common doom), then scepticism, then disbelief, resting at last in manhood's pondering repose of If. But once gone through, we trace the round again; and are infants, boys, and men, and Ifs eternally." *Moby-Dick*, ch. 114, p. 624.

[26] Donald Pizer, "A Primer of Fictional Aesthetics," *College English*, 30 (April 1969), 577.

[27] See Thomas M. Lorch, "The Cyclical Structure of *The Red Badge of Courage*," *CLA Journal*, 10 (March 1967), 229–38.

[28] See John Bass, "How Novelist Crane Acts on the Battlefield," in *The War Dispatches of Stephen Crane*, ed. Stallman and Hagemann, p. 42: "I was curious to know what was passing in his mind, and said:
  'Crane, what impresses you most in this affair?' . . .
  'Between two great armies battling against each other the interesting thing is the mental attitude of the men!' "

[29] There are moments of stress when Crane says that Henry "reflected," but these should probably be distinguished from those occurring in the three moments of extended calm.

[30] Merleau-Ponty, *Themes from the Lectures at the Collège de France, 1962–70*, trans. O'Neill, p. 15.

[31] For example, in the manuscript version of *The Red Badge*, Crane wrote that his apparently deluded protagonist "had been to touch the great death and found that it was but the great death, *and was for others*" (emphasis added). This sounds much like the sentiments after his desertion, when he asks, "how could they kill him who was the chosen of the gods and doomed to greatness?" Deletion of the notion that death "was for others" from the final version seems to indicate that the intention was to reduce the irony of the final chapter.

[32] See Griffith, "The Ironic Last Word," p. 88.

[33] See Rathbun, "Structure and Meaning in *The Red Badge of Courage*," pp. 8–16, and William B. Dillingham, "Insensibility in *The Red Badge of Courage*," *College English*, 25 (December 1963), 194–98.

[34] Quoted in Linson, *My Stephen Crane*, p. 37.

[35] For the short stories under discussion, the text is again the Virginia edition.

[36] See Levenson, *Works* (Virginia), V, lxvii: "Freedom from self and sentimentality affects not only vision but language."

[37] See James B. Colvert, "Style and Meaning in Stephen Crane's 'The Open Boat,' " *University of Texas Studies in English*, 37 (1958), 34–45.

[38] Berryman, *Stephen Crane*, p. 291.

[39] For other examples of the story's intense sensory and perceptual impressions and Crane's means of presenting them, see Andrew Lytle, " 'The Open Boat': A Pagan Tale," *The Hero with the Private Parts*, pp. 60–75, and Charles R. Metzger, "Realistic Devices in Stephen Crane's 'The Open Boat,' " *The Midwest Quarterly*, 4 (Autumn 1962), 50–54.

[40] See Griffith, "The Ironic Last Word," pp. 86–87.

[41] Frank O'Connor, *The Lonely Voice* (rpt., 1968), p. xviii. The general definition is O'Connor's.

[42] O'Faoláin, *The Short Story*, p. 196.

[43] "They both turned to watch him and they remained there deep in reflection, absorbed in contemplation of this wavering figure in the distance, until observation was no longer possible" ("A Lovely Jag in a Crowded Car"). "He resumed his march along the path and the dog walked, tranquilly meditative, at his master's heels" ("The Snake"). "He moved off toward the intense darkness of the village streets" ("A Fishing Village"). "He picked up his starboard revolver, and placing both weapons in their holsters, he went away. His feet made funnel-shaped tracks in the heavy sand" ("The Bride Comes to Yellow Sky").

[44] Crane seems to share this habit with Hawthorne, at least as Hawthorne is described by Jorge Luis Borges: "situations were Hawthorne's stimulus, Hawthorne's point of departure—situations, not characters. Hawthorne first imagined, perhaps unwittingly, a situation and then sought the characters to embody it. I am not a novelist, but I suspect that few novelists have proceeded in that fashion." Borges later remarks that this "method can produce, or tolerate admirable stories . . . but not admirable novels." Borges, "Nathaniel Hawthorne," in *Other Inquisitions* (rpt., 1968), pp. 52–53.

[45] "Introduction," *Works* (Virginia), IV, ix.

[46] Fitzgerald, *The Great Gatsby*, p. 2.

[47] Coleridge, *Biographia Literaria*, p. 12.

CHAPTER 4. A SUITABLE SUBJECT: THE WEST AND THE WESTERNER

[1] "The Bride Comes to Yellow Sky," "The Blue Hotel," and "The Open Boat" are generally considered to be Crane's best short stories. The other Western tales are: "One Dash—Horses," "A Freight Car Incident [A Texas Legend]," "A Man and Some Others," "The Wise Men: A Detail of American Life in Mexico," "The Five White Mice," "Twelve O'Clock," and "Moonlight on the Snow." According to Pizer, *Bibliography*, p. 131, only Eric Solomon's discussion of the Western stories in his "The Gunfighters," in *Parody*, pp. 229–56, has fully treated "this otherwise neglected phase of Crane's writing." The first two stories mentioned are, of course, exceptions, and according to Pizer, "Crane studies would profit from a ten-year moratorium on 'Blue Hotel' explications."

[2] Fussell, *Frontier*.

[3] See Folsom, *The American Western Novel,* p. 13.

[4] See Lee, *From West to East,* p. 154. Lee agrees with Fussell that the six authors studied in *Frontier* "certainly did not have firsthand knowledge of the West." Lee goes on to say that the "first three barely left the eastern seaboard. Of the others, Thoreau had been to Minnesota in 1861, just before his death. Melville had been in 1840 at the age of twenty-one to the Galena lead mines in northern Illinois, on the Mississippi (and from that short acquaintance with the river had written *The Confidence-Man*). Whitman had been, it is supposed, only as far west as New Orleans. All that the six wrote, then, is based on the writings of others or on their own imaginations."

[5] Smith, *Virgin Land,* p. 92.

[6] Solomon, *Parody,* p. 240.   [7] Ibid., p. 243.   [8] Ibid., p. 233.

[9] Bernard DeVoto, "Two Points of a Joke," The Easy Chair, *Harper's Magazine,* Oct. 1951, p. 75.

[10] "Dan Emmonds" in *Complete Short Stories and Sketches,* ed. Gullason, p. 65.

[11] *The Red Badge* is full of similar references. Henry "seemed to shut his eyes and wait to be gobbled" (*RB,* 230). "The enemy would presently swallow the whole command" (*RB,* 217–18). "The brigade was hurrying briskly to be gulped into the infernal mouths of the war god" (*RB,* 232). And while in flight from battle, Henry imagines the men behind him as "initial morsels for the dragons" (*RB,* 231).

[12] See Solomon, *Parody,* pp. 240–41.   [13] Cady, *Stephen Crane,* p. 79.

[14] Quoted in Robert Daley, "The Risk Takers," *Playboy,* June 1969, p. 176.

[15] Stegner, *Wolf Willow,* p. 136.

[16] Wister, *The Virginian* in *Writings,* IV, 22.

[17] See Levenson, "Introduction," *Works* (Virginia), V, xxxix.

[18] Roosevelt, "The Strenuous Life," in *The Strenuous Life: Essays and Addresses,* p. 20.

[19] Kramer, ed., *Lombardi: Winning Is the Only Thing.*

[20] Fitzgerald, "Ring," in *The Crack-Up,* ed. Wilson, p. 37.

[21] DeVoto, "Phäethon on Gunsmoke Trail," The Easy Chair, *Harper's Magazine,* Dec. 1954, p. 16.

[22] See Crane's early sketch, "Not Much of a Hero." Crane treats Tom Quick, a Sullivan County hero in the tradition of Lew Wetzel, in a similar way. Rather than "one of those sturdy and bronzed woodsmen who cleared the path of civilization," Indian fighter Tom Quick is more like Melville's Moredock or even Twain's Slade. Quick is "a man whose hands were stained with unoffending blood, purely and simply a murderer" (VIII, 215).

[23] Smith, *Virgin Land,* pp. 109–10.

[24] Davis, *The West From a Car-Window,* p. 6.

[25] See Robert Barnes, "Stephen Crane's 'The Bride Comes to Yellow Sky,' " *Explicator,* 16 (Apr. 1958) Item 39, and Kenneth Bernard, " 'The Bride Comes to Yellow Sky': History as Elegy," *The English Record,* 17 (Apr. 1967), pp. 17–20.

[26] See Solomon, *Parody,* p. 256.

[27] For discussions of who or what is the cause of the Swede's death, see Joseph N. Satterwhite, "Stephen Crane's 'The Blue Hotel': The Failure of Understanding," *Modern Fiction Studies,* 2 (Winter 1956–1957), 238–41; Walter Sutton, "Pity and Fear in 'The Blue Hotel,'" *American Quarterly,* 4 (Spring 1952), 73–78; and Alan H. Wycherley, "Crane's 'The Blue Hotel,': How Many Collaborators?" *American Notes & Queries,* 4 (Feb. 1966), 88.

[28] For views of the story's conclusion, see James T. Cox, "Stephen Crane as Symbolic Naturalist: An Analysis of 'The Blue Hotel,'" *Modern Fiction Studies,* 3 (Summer 1957), 147–58; William B. Dillingham, "'The Blue Hotel' and the Gentle Reader," *Studies in Short Fiction,* 1 (Spring 1964), 224–26; and Bruce L. Grenberg, "Metaphysics of Despair: Stephen Crane's 'The Blue Hotel,'" *Modern Fiction Studies,* 14 (Summer 1968), 203–13.

CHAPTER 5. THE LIMITS OF CRANE'S ARTISTRY

[1] Kermode, *The Sense of an Ending,* p. 133.

[2] Iris Murdoch, "Salvation by Words," *New York Review of Books,* 15 June 1972, p. 3.

[3] Kermode, *The Sense of an Ending,* pp. 137–38.

[4] Quoted in ibid., p. 152.   [5] Quoted in ibid., p. 127.

[6] Auerbach, *Mimesis,* p. 506.

[7] Auden, "Lame Shadows," *New York Review of Books,* 3 Sept. 1970, pp. 10, 12.

[8] Ellison, "Stephen Crane and the Mainstream of American Fiction," in *Shadow and Act,* pp. 74–88.

[9] Kermode, *The Sense of an Ending,* p. 147.

[10] See Berthoff, *The Ferment of Realism,* pp. 234–35: "What results is of course a kind of idealization. The real itself is not real until it has been glazed into purity."

[11] "Of all human lots for a person of sensibility," Crane wrote of himself, "that of an obscure free lance in literature or journalism is, I think, the most discouraging" (*Letters,* p. 78).

[12] See George W. Johnson, "Stephen Crane's Metaphor of Decorum," *PMLA,* 78 (1963), 256.

[13] *War Dispatches,* ed. Stallman and Hagemann, p. 51.

[14] Hoffman, *Poetry,* p. 278.

[15] Mailer, *Cannibals and Christians,* p. 113.

[16] Pritchett, *The Living Novel,* p. 174.

[17] "Introduction," *Work,* ed. Follett, X. xii.

[18] Ziff, *American 1890s,* p. 191.

[19] Mailer, *Cannibals and Christians,* p. 113.

[20] For the basis of this distinction, see Mirrielees, *Story Writing,* pp. 25–26.

[21] "Review of Nathaniel Hawthorn's *Twice-Told Tales,*" in *The Complete Works of Edgar Allen Poe,* ed. Harrison, XI, 107.

[22] Harold Martin, "Development of Style" in *Style in Prose Fiction,* p. 133.

[23] See ibid., pp. 133–41.

[24] Perry Miller, "The Rhetoric of Sensation," *Errand into the Wilderness*, p. 179.

[25] Tocqueville, *Democracy in America*, ed. Bradley, II, 59.

[26] Emerson, "Circles," *Complete Works*, ed. E. W. Emerson, II, 318.

[27] Hathorn, *Tragedy, Myth, and Mystery*, p. 19.

[28] Perry Miller, "An American Language," *Nature's Nation*, p. 227.

[29] Poe, "Marginalia," *Works*, XVI, 88.

[30] Melville, *The Confidence-Man* (New York: Grove, 1955), p. 94. Subsequent references are to this edition.

[31] Dickinson, *Complete Poems*, ed. Johnson, p. 486.

[32] "A bird came down the walk," in ibid., p. 156.

[33] Ellison, "Stephen Crane and the Main Stream of American Fiction," *Shadow and Act*, p. 81.

[34] Melville, *Letters*, ed. Davis and Gilman, pp. 125 and 277.

[35] Mayhall, "Stephen Crane to the Rescue," *New York Review of Books*, 10 Aug. 1972, p. 28.

[36] Mailer, *The Naked and the Dead*, p. 569. For a discussion of this and other World War II novels and the relationship between men and machines, see Randall H. Waldron, "The Naked, the Dead and the Machine: A New Look at Norman Mailer's First Novel," *PMLA*, 87 (1972), 271–77.

[37] Van Ghent, *The English Novel*, p. 129.

[38] Eliot, *Complete Poems*, p. 12.

[39] Quoted in Stallman, *Biography*, p. 368.

[40] Quoted in ibid., p. 368.

[41] Quoted in ibid., p. 393. Also see pp. 512, 515. As he lay dying Cora Crane wrote, "My husband's brain is never at rest. He lives over everything in dreams and talks aloud constantly. It is too awful to hear him try to change places in the 'Open Boat.' " And in words that could have been those of the correspondent when plunged into the sea, Crane told a friend, "When you come to the hedge that we must all go over, you feel sleepy—and—you don't care."

BIBLIOGRAPHY

———•◆•———

EDITIONS OF CRANE'S WORKS

Bowers, Fredson, ed. *The University of Virginia Edition of the Works of Stephen Crane.* Charlottesville: University Press of Virginia, 1969–. I, *Bowery Tales,* intro. James B. Colvert, 1969. IV, *The O'Ruddy,* intro. J. C. Levenson, 1971. V, *Tales of Adventure,* intro. J. C. Levenson, 1970. VI, *Tales of War,* intro. James B. Colvert, 1970. VII, *Tales of Whilomville,* intro. J. C. Levenson, 1969. VIII, *Tales, Sketches, and Reports,* intro. Edwin H. Cady, 1973. IX, *Reports of War,* intro. James B. Colvert, 1971.

Bradley, Scully, R. C. Beatty, and E. H. Long, eds. *The Red Badge of Courage.* Norton Critical Edition. New York: Norton, 1962.

Follett, Wilson, ed. *The Work of Stephen Crane.* 12 vols. New York: Knopf, 1925–27.

Gullason, Thomas A., ed. *The Complete Novels of Stephen Crane.* Garden City, New York: Doubleday, 1967.

———, ed. *The Complete Short Stories and Sketches of Stephen Crane.* New York: Doubleday, 1963.

Katz, Joseph, ed. *Maggie: A Girl of the Streets . . . A Facsimile Reproduction of the 1893 Edition.* Gainesville: Scholars' Facsimiles and Reprints, 1966.

———, ed. *The Poems of Stephen Crane: A Critical Edition.* Rev. ed. New York: Cooper Square, 1971.

———, ed. *The Portable Stephen Crane.* New York: Viking, 1969.

Lettis, Richard, Robert F. McDonnell, and William E. Morris, eds. *The Red Badge of Courage: Text and Criticism.* New York: Harcourt, Brace, and World, 1960.

Schoberlin, Melvin, ed. *The Sullivan County Sketches of Stephen Crane.* Syracuse: Syracuse University Press, 1959.

Stallman, R. W., ed. *Stephen Crane: An Omnibus.* New York: Knopf, 1952.

Stallman, R. W., and Lillian Gilkes, eds. *Stephen Crane: Letters.* New York: New York University Press, 1960.

Stallman, R. W., and E. R. Hagemann, eds. *The New York City Sketches of Stephen Crane.* New York: New York University Press, 1966.

———, eds. *The War Dispatches of Stephen Crane.* New York: New York University Press, 1964.

CRITICAL WORKS AND OTHER SOURCES

Arlen, Michael J. "Notes on the New Journalism." *Atlantic Monthly,* March 1972, pp. 43–47.

Auden, W. H. *A Certain World: A Commonplace Book.* New York: Viking, 1970.

Auden, W. H. "Lame Shadows." Review of *Tonio Kröger and Other Stories,* by Thomas Mann. *New York Review of Books,* 3 Sept. 1970, pp. 10–13.

Auerbach, Erich, *Mimesis: The Representation of Reality in Western Literature.* Translated by Willard R. Trask. 1953. Reprint, Princeton: Princeton University Press, 1968.

Barnes, Robert. "Stephen Crane's 'The Bride Comes to Yellow Sky.' " *Explicator,* 16 (April 1958), Item 39.

Bassan, Maurice, ed. *Stephen Crane: A Collection of Critical Essays.* Englewood Cliffs, N.J.: Prentice Hall, 1967.

Bernard, Kenneth. " 'The Bride Comes to Yellow Sky': History as Elegy." *The English Record,* 17 (April 1967), 17–20.

Berryman, John. *Stephen Crane.* New York: Sloane, 1950.

Berthoff, Warner. *The Ferment of Realism.* New York: Free Press, 1965.

Borges, Jorge Luis. *Other Inquisitions, 1937–52.* 1964. Reprint, New York: Simon and Schuster, 1968.

Brennan, Joseph X. "Ironic and Symbolic Structure in Crane's *Maggie.*" *Nineteenth-Century Fiction,* 16 (March 1962), 303–15.

Bridgman, Richard. *The Colloquial Style in America.* New York: Oxford University Press, 1966.

Cady, Edwin H. *Stephen Crane.* New York: Twayne, 1962.

Cather, Willa. "When I Knew Stephen Crane." *The Library,* 23 June 1900, pp. 17–18. Reprinted in *Stephen Crane: A Collection of Critical Essays.* Edited by Maurice Bassan. Englewood Cliffs, N.J.: Prentice Hall, 1967, pp. 12–17.

Cazemajou, Jean. *Stephen Crane.* Minneapolis: University of Minnesota Press, 1969.

Coleridge, Samuel Taylor. *Biographia Literaria, or Biographical Sketches of My Literary Life and Opinions.* Edited by George Watson. London: J. M. Dent, 1965.

Colvert, James B. "Stephen Crane's Magic Mountain." In *Stephen Crane: A Collection of Critical Essays.* Edited by Maurice Bassan. Englewood Cliffs, N.J.: Prentice Hall, 1967, pp. 95–105.

——. "Structure and Theme in Stephen Crane's Fiction." *Modern Fiction Studies,* 5 (Autumn 1959), 199–208.

——. "Style and Meaning in Stephen Crane's 'The Open Boat.' " *University of Texas Studies in English,* 37 (1958), 34–45.

Conrad, Joseph. *Last Essays.* Garden City, N.Y.: Doubleday, Doran, 1926.

Cox, James Trammell. "The Imagery of *The Red Badge of Courage.*" *Modern Fiction Studies,* 5 (Autumn 1959), 209–19.

——. "Stephen Crane as Symbolic Naturalist: An Analysis of 'The Blue Hotel.' " *Modern Fiction Studies,* 3 (Summer 1957), 147–58.

Cunliffe, Marcus. "Stephen Crane and the American Background of *Maggie.*" *American Quarterly,* 7 (Spring 1955), 31–44.

Daley, Robert. "The Risk Takers." *Playboy,* June 1969, pp. 141–42, 150, 176–81.

Davis, Richard Harding. *The West From a Car-Window.* New York: Harper, 1892.

DeVoto, Bernard. "Phäethon on Gunsmoke Trail." The Easy Chair #230, *Harper's Magazine,* Dec. 1954, pp. 10–16.

——. "Two Points of a Joke." The Easy Chair #192. *Harper's Magazine,* Oct. 1951, pp. 73–76.

Dickinson, Emily, *Complete Poems.* Edited by Thomas H. Johnson. Boston: Little, Brown, 1960.

Dillingham, William B. " 'The Blue Hotel' and the Gentle Reader." *Studies in Short Fiction*, 1 (Spring 1964), 224–26.

——. "Insensibility in *The Red Badge of Courage.*" *College English*, 25 (December 1963), 194–98.

Eliot, T. S. *The Complete Poems and Plays, 1909–1950*. New York: Harcourt, Brace, and World, 1971.

Ellison, Ralph. *Shadow and Act.* 1964. Reprint, New York: New American, 1966.

Emerson, Ralph Waldo. *Essays: Second Series.* Boston: Houghton, 1886.

——. *Works.* Centenary ed. Vol. II. Boston: Houghton, 1903.

Fitelson, David. "Stephen Crane's *Maggie* and Darwinism." *American Quarterly*, 16 (Summer 1964), 182–84.

Fitzgerald, F. Scott. *The Crack-up.* Edited by Edmund Wilson. 1945. Reprint, New York: New Directions, 1962.

——. *The Great Gatsby.* New York: Scribner, 1925.

Folsom, James K. *The American Western Novel.* New Haven, Conn.: College and University Press, 1966.

Ford, Ford Madox. "Stevie and Company." *New York Herald Tribune Book Supplement*, 2 Jan. 1927, pp. 1 and 6.

——. *Thus to Revisit: Some Reminiscences.* New York: Dutton, 1921.

Forster, E. M. *Aspects of the Novel.* New York: Harcourt, Brace, 1927.

Fussell, Edwin. *Frontier: American Literature and the American West.* Princeton: Princeton University Press, 1965.

Gass, William. *Fiction and the Figures of Life.* New York: Knopf, 1970.

Gordon, Caroline. *How to Read a Novel.* New York: Viking, 1957.

—— and Allan Tate, eds. *The House of Fiction.* New York: Scribner, 1950.

Greenfield, Stanley B. "The Unmistakable Stephen Crane." *PMLA*, 73 (1958), 562–72.

Grenberg, Bruce L. "Metaphysics of Despair: Stephen Crane's 'The Blue Hotel.' " *Modern Fiction Studies*, 14 (Summer 1968), 203–13.

Griffith, Clark. "Stephen Crane and the Ironic Last Word." *Philological Quarterly*, 47 (Jan. 1968), 83–91.

Gullason, Thomas A. "The Significance of *Wounds in the Rain*," *Modern Fiction Studies*, 5 (Autumn 1959), 235–42.

——, ed. *Stephen Crane's Career: Perspectives and Evaluations.* New York: New York University Press, 1972.

Hart, John E. "*The Red Badge of Courage* as Myth and Symbol." *University of Kansas City Review*, 19 (Summer 1952), 249–56.

Hartwick, Harry. *The Foreground of American Fiction.* New York: American Book Co., 1934.

Hathorn, Richmond Y. *Tragedy, Myth and Mystery.* Bloomington: Indiana University Press, 1962.

Hemingway, Ernest. *Death in the Afternoon.* New York: Scribner, 1932.

Hoffman, Daniel G. *The Poetry of Stephen Crane.* New York: Columbia University Press, 1957.

Holton, Milne. *Cylinder of Vision: The Fiction and Journalistic Writing of Stephen Crane.* Baton Rouge: Louisiana State University Press, 1972.

Howells, William Dean. "Life and Letters." *Harper's Weekly*, 25 Jan. 1896, p. 79.

Johnson, George W. "Stephen Crane's Metaphor of Decorum." *PMLA*, 78 (1963), 250–56.

Katz, Joseph. "The *Maggie* Nobody Knows." *Modern Fiction Studies*, 12 (Summer 1966), 200–12.

Kermode, Frank. *The Sense of an Ending: Studies in the Theory of Fiction.* New York: Oxford University Press, 1967.

Kipling, Rudyard. *The Writings in Prose and Verse of Rudyard Kipling.* Vol. IX. New York: Scribner, 1898.

Kramer, Jerry, ed. *Lombardi: Winning Is the Only Thing.* New York: World, 1971.

LaFrance, Marston. *A Reading of Stephen Crane.* New York: Oxford University, 1971.

Leach, Edmund. "Mythical Inequalities." *New York Review of Books*, 28 Jan. 1971, pp. 44–45.

Lee, Robert Edson. *From West to East: Studies in Literature of the American West.* New Haven: College and University Press, 1966.

Liebling, A. J. "The Dollars Damned Him." *The New Yorker*, 5 Aug. 1961, pp. 48–72.

Linson, Corwin Knapp. *My Stephen Crane.* Edited by Edwin H. Cady. Syracuse: Syracuse University Press, 1958.

Lorch, Thomas M. "The Cyclical Structure of *The Red Badge of Courage.*" *CLA Journal*, 10 (March 1967), 229–38. Reprinted in *Stephen Crane's Career: Perspectives and Evaluations.* Edited by Thomas A. Gullason. New York: New York University Press, 1972, pp. 352–60.

Lytle, Andrew. *The Hero with the Private Parts.* Baton Rouge: Louisiana State University Press, 1966.

Mailer, Norman. *Cannibals and Christians.* New York: Dial, 1966.

———. *The Naked and the Dead.* New York: Rinehart, 1948.

Marcus, Mordecai. "The Unity of *The Red Badge of Courage.*" In *Stephen Crane's The Red Badge of Courage: Text and Criticism.* Edited by Richard Lettis, Robert F. McDonnell, and William E. Morris. New York: Harcourt, Brace, 1960, pp. 189–95.

Martin, Harold C. "The Development of Style in Nineteenth-Century American Fiction." In *Style in Prose Fiction: English Institute Essays 1958.* Edited by Harold C. Martin. New York: Columbia University Press, 1959.

Martin, Jay. *Harvests of Change: American Literature, 1865–1914.* Englewood Cliffs, N.J.: Prentice Hall, 1967.

Mayhall, Jane. "Stephen Crane to the Rescue." *New York Review of Books*, 10 Aug. 1972, pp. 28–30.

Melville, Herman. *The Confidence-Man.* New York: Grove, 1955.

———. *Letters.* Edited by Merrell H. Davis and William H. Gilman. New Haven: Yale University Press, 1960.

———. *Moby-Dick.* New York: Bobbs-Merrill, 1964.

Merleau-Ponty, Maurice. *Themes from the Lectures at the Collège de France, 1962–70.* Translated by John O'Neill. Evanston, Ill.: Northwestern University Press, 1970.

Metzger, Charles R. "Realistic Devices in Stephen Crane's 'The Open Boat.' " *The Midwest Quarterly*, 4 (Autumn 1962), 47–54.

Miller, Perry. *Errand into the Wilderness.* 1956. Reprint, New York: Harper and Row, 1964.

———. *Nature's Nation.* Cambridge: Harvard University Press, 1967.

Miller, Ruth. "Regions of Snow: The Poetic Style of Stephen Crane." *Bulletin of the New York Public Library*, 72 (1968), 328–49.

Mirrielees, Edith Ronald, *Story Writing.* New York: Viking, 1962.

Moers, Ellen, "When New York Made It." *New York Times Book Review,* 16 May 1971, pp. 31–32.

Murdoch, Iris. "Salvation by Words." Excerpted from Blashfield Address delivered to American Academy of Arts and Letters, 17 May 1972. *New York Review of Books,* 15 June 1972, pp. 3–6.

Norris, Frank. Review of *Maggie. Wave,* 4 July 1896, p. 13.

O'Connor, Frank. *The Lonely Voice: A Study of the Short Story.* 1963. Reprint, New York: Bantam, 1968.

O'Faoláin, Seán. *The Short Story.* London: Collins, 1948.

Oliver, Arthur. "Jersey Memories—Stephen Crane." *New Jersey Historical Society Proceedings,* n.s. 16 (Oct. 1931), 454–63.

Ortega y Gasset, José. "The Nature of the Novel." Translated by Evelyn Rugg and Diego Marin. *The Hudson Review,* 10 (Spring 1957), pp. 11–42.

Øverland, Orm. "The Impressionism of Stephen Crane: A Study in Style and Technique." *Americana Norvegica.* Edited by Sigmund Skaard and Henry H. Wasser. Philadelphia: University of Pennsylvania Press, 1966. Vol. I, pp. 239–85.

Overmyer, Janet. "The Structure of Crane's *Maggie*." *University of Kansas City Review,* 29 (Autumn 1962), 71–72

Parrington, Vernon L. *Main Currents in American Thought.* Vol. III. New York: Harcourt, Brace, 1930.

Perosa, Sergio. "Naturalism and Impressionism in Stephen Crane's Fiction." Translated by Sergio Perosa. In *Stephen Crane: A Collection of Critical Essays.* Edited by Maurice Bassan. Englewood, N.J.: Prentice Hall, 1967, pp. 80–94.

Pizer, Donald. "A Primer of Fictional Aesthetics." *College English,* 30 (April 1969), 572–80.

——. "Stephen Crane." In *Fifteen American Authors before 1900: Bibliographic Essays on Research and Criticism.* Edited by Robert A. Rees and Earl N. Harbert. Madison: University of Wisconsin Press, 1971, pp. 97–138.

Poe, Edgar Allen. *Works.* Vols. XI and XVI. Edited by James A. Harrison. New York: Cromwell, 1902.

Pritchett, V. S. *The Living Novel.* New York: Reynal and Hitchcock, 1947.

Rahv, Philip. "Fiction and the Criticism of Fiction." *Kenyon Review,* 18 (Spring 1956), 276–99.

Rathbun, John W. "Structure and Meaning in *The Red Badge of Courage*." *Ball State University Forum,* 10 (Winter 1969), 8–16.

Read, Herbert, *English Prose Style.* London: Bell, 1952.

Roosevelt, Theodore, *The Strenuous Life: Essays and Addresses.* New York: Century, 1900.

Rosen, Charles. "Love That Mozart." *New York Review of Books,* 18 May 1972, pp. 15–18.

Rourke, Constance. *American Humor: A Study of the National Character.* 1931. Reprint, New York: Harcourt, Brace, 1953.

Satterwhite, Joseph N. "Stephen Crane's 'The Blue Hotel': The Failure of Understanding." *Modern Fiction Studies,* 2 (Winter 1956–57), 238–41.

Schorer, Mark. "Technique as Discovery." *Hudson Review,* 1 (Spring 1948), 67–87.

Sewall, R. B. "Crane's *The Red Badge of Courage*." *Explicator,* 3 (May 1954), Item 55.

Shattuck, Roger. *The Banquet Years: The Origins of the Avant-Garde in France, 1885 to World War I.* Rev. ed. New York: Knopf-Vintage, 1968.

Smith, Henry Nash. *The Virgin Land: The American West as Symbol and Myth*. Cambridge: Harvard University Press, 1950.

Solomon, Eric. *Stephen Crane: From Parody to Realism*. Cambridge: Harvard University Press, 1966.

Stallman, R. W. "Notes Toward an Analysis of *The Red Badge of Courage*." In *The Red Badge of Courage*. Norton Critical ed. Edited by Scully Bradley, R. C. Beatty, and E. H. Long. New York: Norton, 1962, pp. 248–54.

———. *Stephen Crane: A Biography*. New York: George Braziller, 1968.

Stegner, Wallace. *Wolf Willow: A History, a Story, and a Memory of the Last Plains Frontier*. New York: Viking, 1962.

Sutton, Walter. "Pity and Fear in 'The Blue Hotel.' " *American Quarterly*, 4 (Spring 1952), 73–78.

Talmage, Reverend Thomas de Witt. *Night Sides of City Life*. 1878. Reprinted as *The Night Side of New York Life*. Wakefield: William Nicholson, n.d.

Taylor, Gordon O. *The Passages of Thought: Psychological Representation in the American Novel, 1870–1900*. New York: Oxford University Press, 1969.

Tocqueville, Alexis de. *Democracy in America*. The Henry Reeves text. Vol. II. Edited by Phillips Bradley. New York: Knopf, 1945.

Twain, Mark, *The Works of Mark Twain*. Vol. X. Edited by Albert Bigelow Paine. New York: Harper, 1922–25.

Van Ghent, Dorothy. *The English Novel: Form and Function*. 1953. Reprint, Harper and Row, 1961.

Waggoner, Hyatt H. *American Poets: From the Puritans to the Present*. Boston: Houghton Mifflin, 1968.

Walcutt, Charles C. *American Literary Naturalism: A Divided Stream*. Minneapolis: University of Minnesota Press, 1956.

Waldron, Randall H. "The Naked, the Dead, and the Machine: A New Look at Norman Mailer's First Novel." *PMLA*, 87 (1972), 271–77.

Wells, H. G. "Stephen Crane from an English Standpoint." *North American Review*, 171 (Aug. 1900), 233–42.

Wister, Owen. *The Writings of Owen Wister*. New uniform rev. ed. Vol. IV. New York: Macmillan, 1928.

Woodress, James. *Willa Cather: Her Life and Art*. New York: Pegasus, 1970.

Wycherley, Alan H. "Crane's 'The Blue Hotel': How Many Collaborators?" *American Notes and Queries*, 4 (Feb. 1966), 88.

Ziff, Larzer. *The American 1890s: Life and Times of a Lost Generation*. New York: Viking, 1966.

INDEX